Acclaim for

WENDY LESSER's

The Amateur

"[Lesser] has the gift of enabling the reader to grasp the deeper workings of art forms, both high and low, in the act of describing how they affect her."
—*The New York Times Book Review*

"Perhaps [Lesser's] most remarkable and unconventional feat is to have written an autobiography that is neither an exercise in self-aggrandizement nor in self-embarrassment, but is a work of arresting—almost shocking—modesty and restraint. In addition, it is consistently interesting and surprising."
—Janet Malcolm

"Filled with beautifully chiseled language and lucid observation. . . . Showcases a lively mind, brimming with fascinating perceptions about the world we live in."
—*San Francisco Chronicle*

"*The Amateur* delights the reader with an independence of mind that has almost passed from our cultural scene. . . . With great vitality, Lesser brings her appetite for life into an accounting of her works and days like no other contemporary autobiography."
—Maureen Howard

"*The Amateur* is not a typical memoir. . . . [It] is that rare thing: the story of an intellectual odyssey undertaken by a woman. . . . [Lesser] is a critic to be treasured." —*Los Angeles Times*

WENDY LESSER

The Amateur

Wendy Lesser is the founding editor of *The Threepenny Review* and the author of four previous books; her reviews and essays appear in major newspapers and magazines across the country. She has been awarded fellowships from the National Endowment for the Humanities and the Guggenheim Foundation, and in 1997 she received the Morton Dauwen Zabel Award from the Academy of Arts and Letters. She lives in Berkeley, California, with her husband and son.

The Amateur

The Amateur

AN INDEPENDENT
LIFE OF LETTERS

WENDY LESSER

Vintage Books
A Division of Random House, Inc.
New York

Vintage and colophon are registered trademarks of Random House, Inc.

Photo of Tamara Toumanova on page 184 by George Platt Lynes.
Copyright © Estate of Russell Lynes. Courtesy of Paul Kopeikin Gallery.

The Library of Congress has cataloged the Pantheon edition as follows:
Lesser, Wendy
The amateur : an independent life of letters / Wendy Lesser.
p. cm.

1. Lesser, Wendy. 2. Periodical editors—United States—Biography. 3.
Critics—United States—Biography. 4. Book reviewing—United States. I.
Title.
PN4874.L3785A3 1999
810.9—dc21
[B] 98-26157 CIP

ISBN: 978-0-375-70381-2

Book design by Misha Beletsky

www.vintagebooks.com

Printed in the United States of America

146694632

For my sister, Janna Lesser

CONTENTS

Overture 3

In Washington Square 10

Wish Fulfillment 23

Vocabulary 29

Mr. Jones 39

Thinking Back on Harvard 50

An American in England 61

Consultants 72

Strange Meeting 86

Report on a Site Visit 101

Founding a Magazine 115

Drafted 123

On Philanthropy 137

Out of Academia 157

Dance Lessons 164

Passionate Witness 170

Portrait of a Ballerina 185

A Night at the Opera 195

Ralph 208

The Conversion 218

Chasing Daldry 232

Thom Gunn 240

Elegy for Mario Savio 264

My Imaginary New York Life 270

ACKNOWLEDGMENTS

Fragments of this book, in somewhat different form, have appeared in a variety of places, including the *London Review of Books*, the *New York Times Book Review*, the *Los Angeles Times Magazine*, *San Francisco Focus*, *Two Cities*, *Dance Ink*, and three anthologies: *The State of the Language* (edited by Leonard Michaels and Christopher Ricks), *The Company of Cats* (edited by Michael Rosen), and *Tolstoy's Dictaphone* (edited by Sven Birkerts). I am grateful to the editors of these publications for their encouragement.

My deepest thanks are due to those who made this book possible, and especially to Richard Rizzo, Nicholas Rizzo, Katharine Ogden Michaels, Lisa Michaels, Gloria Loomis, Camille Smith, Dan Frank, and, as always, Arthur Lubow.

The Amateur

OVERTURE

T he autobiographical mode implies the justification of a life, but that is rather hard to do when one is still in the midst of living it. Also, it is not clear exactly what in the life could justify it. The plan you conceived and executed? A laughable chimera, believable only when you are nineteen years old and deciding on a college major. The choices you made? But if they turned out well, you don't necessarily deserve the credit, and if you try to take it, you will merely sound foolish or smug. Do you, in any case, *make* the important choices, or are they thrust on you?

I had this argument recently with a friend who is nearly my age, a theater director who lives in England. Like me, he has been a freelancer all his working life; in other words, his whole career would seem to be a series of choices. Like me, he is married and a parent. He said: You never really make choices—even, or especially, about the big things. I said: Maybe *you* don't, but I am very

3

conscious of having made choices in my life. You can't plan how the choices will turn out; that isn't under your control. But you can certainly make them. Or at least I can. I feel myself doing so all the time.

Of course, whether you approach life in this way is largely determined by your character, and we don't choose our characters. My own character seems to have been remarkably consistent over a lifetime. I think I was born with a sense of an instantaneous connection between the things I perceived in the world and my feelings about those things. I was born with it, and then it was encouraged in me (largely by my mother, who pretty much raised me on her own). I can see the same thing now in my son: he knows right away how he feels about things—there is no gap between perception and response. I wouldn't have thought this was unusual, except that I have detected the absence of it in many people. It mainly takes the form of their not knowing what they want. I almost always know what I want. My only questions are, first, how I might go about getting it, and second, whether it would be good for me to have it (morally or practically or physiologically or psychologically good—I tend to jumble all these things together).

This instantaneous response often makes me difficult, and sometimes makes me stupid. I can be blind to the complicated hesitations and byways of a situation; I am a bit like a tank, running roughshod over everything. This gets me places, but sometimes the subtleties get trampled in the process. I have tried to compensate for this tendency in myself, and life (including, mainly, other people and works of art) has done its best to help me compensate by forcing me to slow down and consider the details.

But despite its difficulties—which, in any case, are mostly difficulties for other people—my character has served me well. It has made me unable to do most of the jobs that seemed available to someone of my age and education (lawyer, academic, high-powered executive), and it has given me something else to do instead. It has made me . . . well, an eighteenth-century man of letters, though one who happens to be female and lives in twentieth-century Berkeley.

My character gave me this, but my character couldn't have done it on its own. Social history helped. I was born into the upwardly mobile, third-generation-from-immigration middle class. Economic history helped, too. I came of age in the 1960s and 1970s, when America was rich enough to spawn people like me, people who made a living on the fringes of the economy by defining a previously nonexistent niche and then occupying it. I don't think it would be possible for someone starting out now to do things in quite the way I have done. The resources simply aren't there.

And if history is one factor, geography is another.

Berkeley, where I have lived since I was twenty-three, is not just the background to my life: it has in many ways shaped that life. Like eighteenth-century London, it is filled with coffeehouses, scruffy artists, notorious law-breakers, and underemployed literary types. This town makes my kind of life seem not only possible but normal. I belong here.

Perhaps I even belong in a more rooted way than most of the people around me, because I was born in California, and so was my father. This crude biographical fact qualifies me for membership in the rather select club of second-generation native Californians. Actually, we can't be all *that* rare; there must be millions of us statewide, especially when you start to count small babies. But among people my age, in my professional and personal circles, I know only two or three who share this background.

Often, people in California think I am from New York. This may be because I am brash, impatient, judgmental, loud, energetic, efficient, pale-skinned, and red-haired—not qualities traditionally associated with laid-back, beach-frequenting Californians. Or it might be because I am Jewish: in Texas, at any rate, I have noticed that "Eastern" or "New York" is used as a code word for "Jewish," and I suspect that the same thing may be true, at a slightly more benign and less conscious level, among nonmetropolitan Californians. Or the confusion may be due to the fact that my mother is from New York, and though she has been trying since her early twenties, when she first arrived on the West Coast, to erase the more conspicuous manners and speech patterns of her natal place, some of its inflections nonetheless got passed along to me. I say "stand on line," for instance, whereas almost every Californian I went to school with said "stand *in* line." And no doubt my brash, impatient, energetic side can be traced to her as well. (My father, though equally judgmental, tends to be more inhibited.)

I have tried for most of my life *not* to be identified with California. Any kind of regionalism, but particularly the brief-historied, long-winded, unremittingly outdoorsy regionalism of the Far West, has always struck me as stultifying. Still, I have lived here all but six years of my life (four of them spent at college in Cambridge, Massachusetts, two more in Cambridge, England) and have become increasingly resigned to the fact that this is where I am always going to live. Yet something in me still wants to resist.

Among the things I resist is the popularly held view of California. This somewhat outlandish vision is perpetrated not solely or even largely by the so-called East Coast media, but by Californians themselves: the movie and television moguls of Hollywood, the journalists and novelists of Marin County, the self-styled inheritors of Raymond Chandler and Joan Didion. Many of these California spokespeople have only recently arrived, and they therefore see what they expect to see: colorful eccentricity, shallow relationships, perfect weather, mindless enjoyment, and the utter absence of any kind of Puritan work ethic. Like all half-true portraits, this one is both annoyingly persistent and persistently annoying. What especially rankles is the implication that, because we live "out west," we are irretrievably cut off from the rest of the country's serious artistic and intellectual culture.

Part of what I bring to my daily life—part of what it means to live in Berkeley, for me—is the continuing sense of a life lived outside California as well as in it. By this I don't just mean I am aware of what is going on in the metropolitan centers (though I do mean that, as well: an eighteenth-century person of letters needs to pay attention to what is happening in the faraway centers of culture, whether they be Edinburgh and Paris or New York and London). What I mean by "outside" is the life that lies beyond my immediate vicinity and my precise point in time. You could call it the life of art. The things that have happened to me in my four decades here in California, and the things that have happened on stage and canvas and screen and paper, are not two separate realms. They are all part of the mixture that has made me what I am. Or so I imagine. It is always possible that I am deluding myself; we Californians have made a specialty of self-delusion. But we have also specialized in certain forms of clarity and directness (you can see it in the

THE AMATEUR

Los Angeles paintings of David Hockney and Richard Diebenkorn, the film criticism of Pauline Kael). The clarity and the self-delusion go hand in hand, support each other, make each other necessary. And I am the child of both traditions.

IN WASHINGTON SQUARE

S ome places are points in a landscape and others are places in the mind. Tucson, for instance, is the former, Hell the latter (though even Tucson, when I cite it this way in the pages of a book, momentarily shifts out of the landscape and into your mind). Many places are both—actual geographical locations with an overlay, or underbelly, of fictional, imagined, spiritual existence. This double life is especially characteristic of large cities. World capitals like New York, London, Paris, and Rome belong not only to their citizens and their tourists but also to the novelists, poets, painters, architects, journalists, playwrights, and filmmakers who have inhabited and borrowed them. A Henry James character, remarking on his "latent preparedness" for a visit to London, recalls: "I had seen the coffee-room of the Red Lion years ago, at home—at Saragossa, Illinois—in books, in visions, in dreams, in Dickens, in Smollett, in Boswell."

Cities hold on to the events that have taken place in them and the novels that have been written about them. Each urban crevice stores up this radioactive material and gradually leaks it out to successive generations. Especially if you live in an old city, you will be conscious not only of the many other lives led alongside your own but also of the past and future lives crowding in. Far from diluting the effect of your own experience, this crowded history will strengthen each present event: the cracked sidewalks and porous building materials will store up your life and give it forth to you in a way that the smooth walls of a New Town or a planned city never could. For people who live in older cities, the distinction between a place in the landscape and a place in the mind is impossible to make.

You are lucky—or, let us say, your life will more easily make sense to you—if the place in which you live and the language you speak have some inherent connection to each other. I do not just mean that it is hard to be an exile, though in a broader sense perhaps that is exactly what I do mean. America, for instance, is a country full of exiles. Its language was developed in a small, close-knit society, with words that applied to the everyday features of a circumscribed island life; and this language, transplanted from Britain, was then supposed to be adequate to describe a vast continent filled with strange geographies and peopled by numerous different strands of humanity. The language couldn't really do this: it had to stretch, and sometimes break, to cover its new ground. The result is that American literature tends to be quite abstract in comparison to the concreteness of English literature. Think of our nineteenth-century Transcendentalists and Britain's social novelists, our serious-minded experimenters and their witty explorers of the "conventional" and the "real." Think of *Moby-Dick* and *Middlemarch*.

For an American living west of the Mississippi, this alienation from the sources of the language is still more extreme. Our town names, like Los Angeles architecture, seem mere parodies of themselves: Albany, California, is not even Albany, New York, much less the original Duke's Albany or his even more ancient country, Albion. The names we Californians give our things and places are echoes, and these imaginative echoes all seem to come from two removes elsewhere. "Gloucester" is merely a cheese I can buy at the local foodstore; it has no concrete connection to a town in England or even Massachusetts.

This kind of displacement often leads to an elevation of the imaginative connections over the real. When I buy my Gloucester cheese in Berkeley, I think of neither the place in England where it originated nor the town in New England that borrows the name, but the Earl who fathered Edgar and Edmund in *King Lear*. My cheese skips its geographical heritage and goes straight to the literary sources that have become, *ex post facto*, its ancestors. One is likely, under such circumstances, to forget about the chronological transmission of culture and believe instead in a kind of all-encompassing literary unconscious. The problem is similar to that described by Emerson in relation to architecture. "The American who has been confined, in his own country, to the sight of buildings designed after foreign models," he says, "is surprised on entering York Minster or St. Peter's at Rome by the feeling that these structures are imitations also—faint copies of an invisible archetype."

A further sense of removal from the sources of meaning afflicts those who, like me, were brought up in the suburbs. Our literary memories, in English, are mostly those of urban places: primarily London, secondarily New York and Boston. In America one also has a backup set of memories provided by the pioneer or rural literature of James Fenimore Cooper, Mark Twain, Willa Cather, and others. But for the child of the suburbs, there is no imaginative echo surrounding real places, no literary ancestry infusing the objects of everyday life. Especially for the California suburbanite, there is a distinct separation between the real and the fictional—between the swimming pools, shopping centers, cyclone fences, and one-story ranch-style houses that constitute existence, and the "bleak houses," "New Grub Streets," and "Bostonians" that constitute literature.

As a denizen of the California suburbs, I grew up feeling the absence of something, knowing that a deeper layer of significance *ought* to lie behind the flatness of my surroundings. My first response to this longing was to immerse myself in science fiction, which made up the bulk of my reading from age ten to age sixteen. This, if it did not give me literary echoes, at least gave me the sense that hidden meanings enriched everyday objects. The reason much science fiction seems banal is that it is so obviously a search for significance. It projects our daily life or our current technologies onto an unknown future or an alien planet, and thereby asks for ultimate causes, ultimate meanings. Science fiction is the opiate of the atheists. It gives those who believe in rationality the assurance that something larger than randomness or human ineptness is at the root of our existence. Coincidence rationalized into pattern is the essence of science fiction; we who can find no rational connections in our disjunctive daily lives are thereby persuaded that understanding is simply a matter of seeking out the missing pieces.

I should say a word about how I started reading science fiction. My parents were divorced when I was six. My father, who until then had worked in the San Jose office of IBM, took a job with the New York branch and moved east; my mother, my younger sister, and I stayed in the three-bedroom, linoleum-tiled, flat-roofed Palo

Alto tract house my parents had bought when I was three. (Tract house perhaps conveys the wrong impression: these redwood-frame houses, called "Eichlers" after their designer and builder, were manufactured *en masse* in the 1950s as starter homes for aspiring young suburbanites, but they were—and still are—considered nice properties, and the one my parents bought in the Greenmeadow subdivision for $20,000 in 1955 would today sell for about $500,000.) When my father moved out, he left behind in the two-car garage a conglomeration of assorted possessions that he apparently could not bring himself either to dispose of or to take with him. Among these were five copies of a magazine called *Unknown Worlds*, vintage 1942.

I can still remember the crackly feel of the old paper and the monochrome look—olive green, I think—of the black-printed covers. I discovered these magazines the summer I was ten, and I spent a large portion of that summer avidly reading and rereading them. Some of the stories were by Fritz Leiber, Theodore Sturgeon, and other people who went on to science fiction fame; several, amazingly, were written by L. Ron Hubbard (though I didn't know enough then to be amazed); many of my favorites were by someone with the unlikely name of L. Sprague de Camp. I would lie on my bed on a hot summer afternoon and read *Unknown Worlds* until I was too terrified to be alone any longer. Then, dazed with the effort of getting up too suddenly, I would wander out onto the sunlit, grass-lined, clean, new streets of nearly identical Eichlers, and even the shadowless world of Greenmeadow, populated by my friends and neighbors, would seem to emanate some of the lurid uncanniness I had absorbed from my reading. When my father came on one of his semiannual visits, I asked him whether the magazine still existed, and if so, whether I could have a subscription. But *Unknown Worlds* had long since gone out of business, so he bought me instead a five-year subscription (one year at a time: my father is generous but never extravagant) to a monthly called *Fantasy and Science Fiction*.

Two things broke me of science fiction. The possibility of drawing together the imaginary and the real, of finding places in the mind that were also places on earth, was first shown to me by "real" novels and by cities. And because I was a suburban child, the city itself was a novel to me: a place where miraculously diverse characters acted out their unknown and therefore fascinating fates on a seemingly limitless stage.

My first city was San Francisco. However young and small it may seem by comparison to European or East Coast capitals, it was more than enough of a city for me. I remember the zeal with which I decided I would *learn* the city—by observing where the Number 30 bus went, by figuring out the order and direction of Clay, Washington, Jackson, Pacific, and most of all by walking everywhere. Instead of attending classes during my last semester of high school, I persuaded the school authorities to let me take an unpaid job in San Francisco. (Since the job was for a firm of city planners, my employment was deemed sufficiently educational to replace my lost semester, but my father couldn't get over the fact that I was working for no pay. In a way, he was right to worry: it was to become a lifelong bad habit.) I spent most of my lunch hours, and quite a few of my supposed work hours, walking through San Francisco's various neighborhoods. Each house I passed became *my* house, each view my own private discovery. My first sense of the city was therefore intimately linked with a feeling of possession.

Yet a city only really becomes your own when you let go of it a little. The special quality of both cities *and* novels is that they are enriched by previous use, handed to you by others, made intimate by your awareness of their vastness. Both the novel and the city live by projection: immersing yourself in a crowd of characters or citizens, you become defined in relation to them; you lose yourself to find yourself. The city was not something I could take home, like a product in a suburban shopping mall. It was only mine as long as I left it in place. And so the owner had to give way to the observer. Meanwhile, a similar thing was happening to my novel-reading. I began by demanding identification, by wanting to be the characters or have them be me. I didn't like novels about alien personalities. Emma Woodhouse was a pill, Sonia Marmeladov a pathetic martyr, Adam Bede a stuffed shirt, and Esther Summerson was too smirkingly self-effacing to be borne. Every novel, then, was judged by how strongly it made me sympathize with its central characters. Since I was sixteen years old and had spent my entire childhood in redwood-framed suburban comfort, this didn't leave much to identify with.

But as I gained the city by beginning to let go of it, I also began to give literature a longer rein. It was not that I grew to like Esther Summerson (does anyone?) but rather that I came to understand the value of *not* liking her. That a world could be alien to me and still mine—that empathy was a hard-won claim and not an easy virtue—was something that both novels and cities could teach me.

And finally they were also able to teach me their own limits. Eventually I learned that San Francisco was not the only city, and that its Washington Square—the broad expanse of bench-lined lawn in front of Saints Peter and Paul Church in North Beach—was a mere shadow of the "real" Washington Square, the one in Greenwich Village. And even this New York Washington Square was by now a faded reality beside the fictions it had generated: the beatnik hangout, the playground for Grace Paley's mothers and children, the locus of Thirties intellectual strolls, and most of all the title of a novel by Henry James.

Washington Square is the type of novel I would have hated when I was sixteen. The heroine, Catherine Sloper, is a frumpy, somewhat slow, exceedingly sweet-tempered girl who is caught between a stern father and a sleazy beau, neither of whom really loves her. She is not the kind of character one would want to identify with in the first place, and the likelihood of identification is made even smaller by the poor little fate she ends up with in this novel. If the novel is supposed to be about sympathy, it is maudlin; if it is about irony, it is cruel. Yet *Washington Square* is finally neither maudlin nor cruel, and one must therefore conclude that the novel, like the city from which it draws its name, gains its meaning from something other than the easy substitution of one human being for another. In fact, the best novels, like cities, emphasize the impossibility of such substitutions: they reveal the difficulty of feeling empathy in the face of the strongest demands for it. *Washington Square* is about the severe limits on one person's ability to feel for and judge on behalf of another—and it is also about our innate desire to see others as mere projections of ourselves.

Nowhere in the novel is this conflict exhibited more strongly than in James's description of the Square itself. "I know not whether it is owing to the tenderness of early associations," he says,

> but this portion of New York appears to many persons the most delectable. It has the kind of established repose

which is not of frequent occurrence in other quarters of
the long, shrill city; it has a riper, richer, more honourable
look than any of the upper ramifications of the great lon-
gitudinal thoroughfare—the look of having had something of a social history. It was here, as you might have
been informed on good authority, that you had come into
a world which appeared to offer a variety of sources of
interest; it was here that your grandmother lived, in venerable solitude, and dispensed a hospitality which com-
mended itself alike to the infant imagination and the
infant palate; it was here that you took your first walks
abroad, following the nursery-maid with unequal step,
and sniffing up the strange odour of the ailanthus-trees
which at that time formed the principal umbrage of the
Square, and diffused an aroma that you were not yet critical enough to dislike as it deserved; it was here, finally,
that your first school, kept by a broad-bosomed, broad-
based old lady with a ferule, who was always having tea
in a blue cup, with a saucer that didn't match, enlarged
the circle both of your observations and your sensations.

And by this time we have become Henry James. The
twentieth-century child of the California suburbs is expected to "remember" this childhood of nursery maids
and blue teacups. The process of projection is seemingly
complete and apparently unthinking: "you" the reader
have quite naturally evolved into the author, whose own

"early assocations" were precisely those of the upper-class Washington Square existence. Yet the transformation is neither complete nor unthinking, for just as you have begun to take possession of this fictional childhood memory, Henry James interrupts you with the final line of his description: "It was here, at any rate, that my heroine spent many years of her life; which is my excuse for this topographical parenthesis." The vividly remembered Washington Square has become a mere "topographical parenthesis" in a novel, the "heroine" of which is precisely *not* the sort of person into whom one can comfortably project oneself. The illusion of projection, in other words, has been shattered by a reminder that we aren't all the same person, and that novels aren't life.

If this is a sad reminder, it is also a relief. Henry James would be the first to admit that novels can limit life as much as they can enrich it. And sometimes the sober realizations that novels impose on us, such as the awareness that people can never truly identify with each other, or that life is a matter of alienation, isolation, and false projection, get temporarily wiped out by an unexpected urban event. I am thinking in particular of something that happened once in Washington Square—*my* Washington Square, the one in San Francisco.

It was a warm Sunday afternoon during the month of June. I was passing by the Square on one of my habitual walks through the city, and the usual assortment of ancient Asian couples, Italian families, aging flower children, and miscellaneous other San Franciscans were disporting themselves on the grass. As I glanced over the park, I noticed that two raggedly dressed, heavy-set men, apparently drunk, had begun to fight. Actually, it was hardly a fight, but rather a case of the tougher man picking on the weaker one, in the manner of a playground bully. The tough guy pulled off the weak one's shirt and strolled away with it, leaving his victim looking helpless and pathetic (as one does when violently deprived of clothing in a public place). And then, just as I had decided the whole disturbing incident was over, a man in a knit cap—a longshoreman, from the looks of him—who had been standing with an entirely different group in the park, left his friends and headed toward the tough guy. Now, I thought, *they'll* start to fight. But the longshoreman just took the shirt away, walked over to the weaker drunk, and handed it back to him—an act of pure and gratuitous kindness, following from nothing and leading nowhere. The longshoreman went back to his friends and I continued on my walk, pleased that for once the city had violated my novelistic notions of causality, projection, motive, and pattern.

WISH FULFILLMENT

For those of us who love Dickens, the need for him goes very deep, as if it were a primal urge, or a deeply buried childhood memory waiting to be touched upon and reawakened. In my case, at least, he *is* a childhood memory. One of my earliest literary remembrances is of my mother reading aloud the whole of *David Copperfield* to my six-year-old sister and my eight-year-old self. These readings always took place on the couch in our living room (the same couch in whose cushions I had once hidden my little sister's favorite blanket and then, in my typically cavalier and reprehensible way, forgotten all about it, so that it stayed lost for months). My sister and I would sit on either side of our mother as she held the book in her lap. Sometimes I would glance over at the words on the page, but more often I would just stare off into the distance and listen. I could already read to myself, of course, and less than two years later I would attempt *A Tale of Two Cities* on my own (and repeatedly attempt it, four or five times, until I finally got past that obscure and contrary first paragraph). But this was different from reading to oneself. This was immersion.

Sometimes my mother would stop to weep at a particularly sad passage—the death of David's mother, for instance, or the much later death of Dora—and I would demand impatiently, "Why are you stopping? Keep reading!" This was not just the impatience of an eight-year-old to hear the rest of the story (although it was in part that: patience has never been one of my virtues). It was also the distress—I would even say the resentment—of a child confronted with an adult's tears. And in my case the normal childish distress (*Who will keep me safe from sadness if even the adults are crying?*) was augmented by a feeling that my mother's tears were a rebuke to me. She and my sister were sensitive, I was hardhearted: that is how she had defined our emotional territory, or so I believed. "When we told you about the divorce, your sister cried but you didn't," my mother had reminded me more than once. Perhaps she only meant it as an invitation to express my sadness, but I took it as a criticism of my capacity for feeling.

A Berkeley friend of mine reports a related but opposite incident from his own life. When he first got divorced, his three young children would come to stay with him on occasional visits, and he decided it would be nice to read *David Copperfield* to them, as it had been read aloud to him when he was young. But after a few chapters his youngest daughter, who was then four, asked him if he could please stop: it was too much for her, all this intense material about childhood and loss. "It was like mainlining emotion," says my friend, making a gesture that suggests a hypodermic applied to his inner arm.

I envy and admire that little girl's willingness to admit her feelings of loss. Such confessions have never come easily to me—least of all when dealing with a parent (least of *all* when dealing with a father). And I agree with my friend's assessment of the situation, which is also an assessment of Dickens's appeal. But what makes that appeal unique is the way we are allowed to absorb all of Dickens's emotionality—gorge ourselves on the sentiment, wallow in the occasional silliness, long for a happy ending, and eventually get our wish—yet still feel clean and free at the end. Most sentimental writing leaves you sick to your stomach, so that you feel sated but sullied when you reach the end of it; and most novels that give you exactly what you think you want (the average mystery, for example) leave you with a terrible sense of letdown—with the discovery that what you thought you desired isn't satisfying after all. But Dickens never disappoints in this way. He gives you more than you imagined you wanted. He wounds you and then he soothes you, but he leaves you with a residue of what it felt like to be wounded, a tangy bitterness that cleanses the sweetness of the happy ending.

If you feel this way about Dickens, you never get over the fact that you have exhausted all the available novels by him. It's all very well to reread *David Copperfield* every few years (well, better than all very well: it's marvelous), but there remains an appetite for new material that is not appeased by these old satisfactions. Whenever I'm in an unfamiliar bookstore, I find myself unwittingly looking under the "D's," irrationally hoping that I'll be surprised by a new Dickens novel.

For a long time I had half a novel left. I kept *The Mystery of Edwin Drood* for last because I knew how I would suffer when I reached the last page Dickens had written. To the usual distress one experiences when a mystery novel is lost in mid-read (the acute anxiety about how it all turned out, the immediate concern about being able to buy or borrow a replacement copy, the outright desperation to know the end) would be added all the despair of being ripped untimely from the warm, dark, soothing-dreadful hideaway created by Dickens's language. I wasn't sure I could stand this feeling. But I was perpetually tempted. Finally, when I was in my early thirties, I gave in and read the unfinished novel.

I can still remember the horrible feeling that came over me when I reached the last words of Dickens's version ("and then falls to with an appetite"). In my edition,

Edwin Drood came packaged with *Master Humphrey's Clock* appended to it, so I didn't even have the warning signal of the pages dwindling to an end: I was reading happily along in a volume that still had plenty of pages left in it, and then, turning a page, I was suddenly ejected from the story. I was lying in the bathtub (where I do some of my best reading) and I groaned aloud—such a serious groan that my husband anxiously called out, "What's the matter?" It was impossible to explain the full extent of what was the matter; it seemed foolish to be so disappointed by something I had known perfectly well was going to happen.

In my willful, wishful dream, I am back in that bathtub and the pages go on and on, to the end of the story as Dickens would have written it. The sentences after "appetite" are all written in the same rich, hilarious, enveloping, convoluted Dickensian prose as the rest of the book; this is no patched-together finishing-up job by a diligent scholar, but the thing itself. And as I read this Real Thing, I realize that I don't care all that much about how the mystery turns out: I don't care, ultimately, whether my feeble guesses in midstream proved to be right or wrong. What I care about is that Dickens finally had the chance to shape the novel to his (and my) satisfaction. "The novel is significant, therefore," said Walter Benjamin, in one of my favorite quotations of all time, "not because it presents someone else's fate to us, perhaps didactically, but because this stranger's fate by virtue of the flame which consumes it yields us the warmth which we never draw from our own fate. What draws the reader to the novel is the hope of warming his shivering life with a death he reads about." That is why my dream wants to replace the incompletion imposed by the novelist's death with the completion offered by the novel's.

VOCABULARY

I t is a common narcissistic fantasy to believe that the world as one knows it started with one's birth, and that prior to one's own appearance all was darkness and antiquity. My particular generation—located at the heart of the baby boomers, midway between Bill Clinton and Madonna—has taken this tendency to an extreme. Thus we would be likely to believe that no one before us had ever argued for school desegregation, worried about the apolitical masses, lived in split-level houses, used automated tools, got sick because of mislabeling, got well because of tetracycline, slept on Posturepedic beds, favored clitorial sex, laughed at Scientologists, mocked Interpol, complained about wolf-whistles, turned from the vomitous rubberiness of pallid U.S. cooking to the pleasures of tapenade, consumed hallucinogenic drugs, taken over multi-use college buildings to protest unjust wars, or elsewhere indulged in a widespread habit of fervent, loud, public gabbiness.

And, lexicographically speaking, we would be right, for every word of over two syllables used in that last sentence first entered the English language in 1952, the year I was born. You might have had some of those thoughts in 1951 or earlier, but you would not, apparently, have been able to express them in precisely those terms. The words that were to define "modern life" for my generation arrived on the scene just as we did.

Or so says my OED on CD-ROM, a toy I acquired mainly to pursue this kind of tantalizing if pointless personal-cum-sociological inquiry. Of course, the game requires that you place firm faith in the OED's dating procedures, and that's not always easy to do when you can *almost* remember using the word before they found it in print. Still, if you give them the benefit of the doubt and agree to accept the OED's 1952 dates as readily as you do those for, say, 1592, you can draw some amazing conclusions about the extent to which language not only reflects but actually forecasts our daily existence.

I use the plural possessive "our" advisedly, for nothing makes you more aware of your inclusion in a cultural generation than looking at your birth-year words in this way. (Or at least *my* birth-year words: I tried the experiment for several friends born in the 1940s and 1960s, and the results weren't nearly as interesting.) What I had thought was personal experience, peculiar to me, turns out to have belonged to my entire age bracket. We did not just employ our birthright words, on an individual basis—we *became* them, as a group.

A related notion struck me a few years back when I attended a design and architecture show at the Whitney Museum in New York. Billed as an exhibit about the 1950s, the show contained a disproportionate number of items I had associated with my particular family life. In one corner were the molded plywood Charles Eames chairs from our living room; in another the brightly hued formica countertops from our kitchen. They even had a scale model of an Eichler house, complete with back patio and sliding glass doors. I had thought I was from a very unusual background, but there at the Whitney I found my childhood writ large, and it turned out to be all of America's.

The 1952 words listed by the OED rang a similar note of uncanny familiarity. They were the linguistic architecture, you might say, surrounding the early years of everyone my age. But in this case the situation was even stranger. It was as if the house we were collectively to occupy had been built at the time of our birth and had waited—completely furnished, not a speck of dust in sight, every appliance fully operational—for us to move in years later, as we grew toward adulthood. Who would have guessed, for example, that the word *hallucinogenic* entered the language as early as 1952? The Summer of Love, after all, didn't take place until 1967. It's odd to think that all those Day-Glo-colored, acid-trip-inspired posters, all those strobe-lighted happenings and Timothy-Leary-esque pronouncements, were gathered there in embryo, like wishes breathed over our collective cradle, waiting until we were old enough to take advantage of them.

Strange, too, that *hallucinogenic* should appear in the dictionary the same year as *beat generation*, the about-to-be-new already prepared to take over from the not-yet-old; or, in a similar vein, that *desegregate* should arise alongside *apolitical*, or *Ms.* come hand-in-hand with *wolf-whistle*. Did anyone, in 1952, even *imagine* asking to be called Ms. instead of Mrs. or Miss? And yet there it is, drawn from a publication called *The Simple Letter* put out by the National Office Management Association in Philadelphia. "Use abbreviation Ms. for *all* women addressees," the *Letter* proposes with wide-eyed if restrained enthusiasm. "This modern style solves an age-old problem." Eventually, maybe. But that was the last we were to hear of this solution until about 1970, when the OED locates it again in, of all places, the *Daily Telegraph*.

I have to say that the OED's choice of sources for its newly evolving words sometimes verges on the idiosyncratic, if not the downright eccentric. The *Economist*, for instance, would seem from the number of its citations to be on the cutting edge of lexical adventurousness. We also get early quotations from the *Guardian*, the *New*

York Times, and the venerable London *Times*—periodicals not usually known for their instant investment in neologisms. On the other hand, the OED readily acknowledges that the *really* new words often come from poets, novelists, and essayists. In 1952, Ernest Hemingway was the first to weigh in with *rubberiness,* Mary McCarthy provided *apolitical,* Norman Mailer came up with *porno* (natch), the film critic Stanley Kauffmann originated both *gabbiness* and *vomitous,* and John Betjeman was the first and, indeed, the only person ever to use the word *plung* (which the OED defines as "a resonant noise as of a tennis racket striking a ball" and categorizes, with hilarious understatement, as "rare"). In general, 1952 was a good year for onomatopoeia: in addition to the Betjeman noise, it gave us *boing, clonk, whomp,* and *thunk* (this last only in the sense of "a sound of an impact, either dull or plangent"; in its earlier non-onomatopoetic sense, as the past tense or noun form of the verb *think,* it had already been used by James Joyce in both *Ulysses* and *Finnegans Wake*).

But not all the words that entered our dictionary for the first time in 1952 were new to the world. Some were just persistent border-crossers. Among these were *tapenade* (which, like *hallucinogenic,* had to wait decades to escape from the specialist manuals into more general menu-driven use), *wok* (whose earliest English incarnation was spelled *wock*), and *don* (in the Italian sense of a

Mafia leader). I originally thought *scuba* must belong in this company (its linguistic texture, not to mention its subject matter, struck me as distinctively Hawaiian, or perhaps Mediterranean), but this now-common noun turns out to have started life as an acronym for Self-Contained Underwater Breathing Apparatus. *Interpol* too is an abbreviation (for International Criminal Police Commission), and why it took from its founding in 1923 to the early 1950s to get itself into the OED is one of those mysteries that its own agents are perhaps best qualified to solve. It is, for me, one of several words in this set that evoke with particular intensity the America of my youth—the America of Alfred Hitchcock thrills and Joseph McCarthy terrors, of *tumble-driers, split-level* homes, and car or bicycle *decals.*

Like *decal,* which first appeared in a journal called *Electronic Engineering,* a number of the era's trademark phrases took a while to emerge from the ghetto of technical obscurity. *Xerox* literally began as a trademark (listed by the U.S. Patent Office in 1952), and so did *Posturepedic,* but in the 1960s both were showing up regularly in newspaper ads and articles; and by 1977, when the Posturepedic mattress slipped casually into literature (in Cyra McFadden's *The Serial,* a send-up of Marin County's sybarites), the xerox copy had become so ubiquitous as to lose, at least in daily usage, its proprietary capital. Some terms, however, never made it past that early stage. *Vinylon*, for instance, failed to get beyond the pages of the *Encyclopedia of Chemical Technology* and the *Textile Research Journal*, though its inventors obviously hoped it would rival its two parents, vinyl and nylon, as a household word. *Stuccadore*, while it seems an efficient way to classify workers in stucco, hasn't been heard from since 1978. The one I'm sorriest to have lost is *peepie-creepie*, which I think perfectly describes the sad, appealing, murderous voyeur in Michael Powell's famous thriller, *Peeping Tom*, though the OED instead defines it as "a portable television camera used for close shots on location."

Television was a new phenomenon in 1952, and computers were barely visible on the horizon. Yet a number of the words we have come to associate with these machines—*downtime, out of series, correlational*, and others of that ilk—were ready and waiting to be used. Of these, the most interesting is *scheduler*, which now has both a television meaning (a recent *New York Times* article referred to network schedulers as the "stuntmen" of the industry, because they pull off so many hair-raising tricks in their efforts to defeat rival programming) and a computer meaning (the OED's second definition is "a machine, esp. a computer, that can arrange a number of planned activities in the order in which they should take place"). What strikes me as significant about this noun is the way it finally attributes agency to what had been viewed since the mid-nineteenth century as a passively experienced condition. Though the word *schedule* (meaning something written on paper) had been around for centuries, its time-table sense didn't arise until shortly after the development of passenger trains, and that's when the verb came into being as well. Beginning with its first appearance in 1862, virtually all the examples cited by the OED put the verb in its passive form: trains, trials, and tennis matches are all scheduled by undesignated, mysterious agents, and even an archbishop who "is scheduled to speak at the Academy of Music" seems to have no contact with the Higher Powers that do the scheduling. Only with the computer age do we discover the thing that actually does the scheduling; and only when this action has been assigned to machines can we, in due course, also attribute it to people.

If 1952 marked an era of regimentation (*off-limits* is another new phrase from that year), it also had its frivolous side. Bernard Malamud gave us the adjective *nyloned* to describe a sexy woman's stocking-clad legs. People under thirteen years of age went from being children to being *subteens*, with their own consumer clout and their own dating patterns. *Partyness* came in as a noun—but wait, no, that's another trend entirely, for *partyness* was apparently a direct transliteration from Lenin's *partiinost*, referring to a Marxist sense of allegiance to the Party. This was no doubt the kind of language Mr. Milton A. Smith was trying to defeat when, in his capacity as assistant general counsel for the American Chamber of Commerce, he coined the word *bafflegab* to describe confusing official jargon. Unfortunately for Mr. Smith, his word succumbed to its own disease, leaving the perfectly good *gobbledygook* (introduced a few years earlier, in 1944) to do its work.

Some of my birthright words seem impossible to have done without for the first half of the twentieth century. How is it that *automate* only emerged in 1952, when machines had already been doing human labor for decades if not centuries? And how did we manage to do without *tee-off*, given that golfing and its verb *to tee* had been around since the eighteenth century? Why did *rubberiness* have to wait for Hemingway, when Galsworthy came up with *rubbery* in 1907 and *rubber* itself, as a shortened form of the plant product *India-rubber*, dates back to 1855? If *gabby* has been an adjective since 1719, and *gab* a noun since 1300, why did we need Stanley Kauffmann to give us *gabbiness*?

Other words, though, I wish we *had* done without. Even before checking the citations, I got chills when I read the word *megaton*. (My chills, however, can't always be trusted: I also got them from the word *pre-nuclear*, but that turns out to be a grammatical term, with no reference whatsoever to bombs.) *Provirus*, with its antiphonal pre-echo of the AIDS-connected retrovirus, also made me nervous. But the word that, when I looked it up, yielded the deepest and most unexpected melancholy was the odd little word *hoochie*. At first I assumed it was another onomatopoetic sound, or else (in concert with *coochie*, perhaps) part of a sweetly dated phrase, like the charming *peepie-creepie*. But when I read the definition, I discovered it was military slang for an insubstantial or temporary shelter or dwelling, probably of Asian origin: in other words, a hootch. That word I recognized. So I was no longer surprised—only saddened, appalled, ashamed even after all these years—when I got to the 1969 citation from *Time* magazine: "Calley's men in less than 20 minutes ignited 'hootches' and chased all the villagers . . . into groups, and shot everyone." That too is part of my generation's collective vocabulary.

MR. JONES

I n the Palo Alto of my childhood, all the public schools were named after California Indian tribes or educational administrators from Stanford. I went to Ohlones Elementary School, Ray Lyman Wilbur Junior High School, and Cubberley (I don't remember his first two names) Senior High School. Anyone from Palo Alto could have told you this probably meant my father worked in the electronics industry—that's the part of town those schools encompassed—and indeed he did, though he happened to commute to San Jose rather than working locally at Philco or Varian or one of the other forerunners of what eventually became Silicon Valley. If I had gone instead to Terman and Gunn, the probabilities would have favored my being a Stanford professor's child; at Jordan and "Paly," I would most likely have come from an old Palo Alto professional family. Since my mother and sister and I stayed on in the same house after my parents split up, I was able, through somewhat devious means, to continue blending in with my surroundings. That is, to questions about what my father did for a living I could give a credible and appropriate answer ("He works for IBM"), even though he was no longer actually present.

At the time, our public school district was reputed to be one of the best in the country (Bethesda, Maryland, I recall, was another). From the point of view of those who keep such statistics, this meant that we got higher-than-average test scores, learned New Math before the rest of the nation, and so on. But to me, both then and in retrospect, it meant that I had a series of memorable, unconventional teachers.

Mr. Schneider, for instance, was my math teacher in seventh and eighth grades. Six foot six and bulky of build, with horn-rimmed glasses and close-cropped hair, he taught mathematics with the enthusiasm of a cheerleader and the force of a heavy-equipment operator. Once, I remember, he told us that the quadratic equation had saved his life. "When I went into the Air Force, I had to take an exam," he said. "And because I could remember the quadratic equation, I got most of the answers in the math section right. And because of that, I ended up a navigator instead of a tail-gunner. And that's why I'm here to tell the tale." I don't remember what war Mr. Schneider was in—it must have been the Korean—but I still remember $(a + b)(a + b) = a^2 + 2ab + b^2$. The chances of my ever having to qualify for a navigator's position have always been rather remote, and they grow more so as I grow older, but Mr. Schneider succeeded in putting the fear of God into me.

In high school there was Mr. Chanteloupe, the apple-cheeked history teacher who was notable mainly for his Catholicism (most teachers didn't admit to a religion) and for his open support of the war in Vietnam. And there was Mr. Jadwin, the Montgomery Clift lookalike who taught sophomore and junior English, supervised the literary magazine, and labored under the crushes of all the sensitive girls. My own favorite was Mr. Gamez, a Spanish teacher who had been born in California—his *grandmother*, he told us, had been born in California—but who nonetheless sported a heavy Mexican accent. He was a good Spanish teacher (a number of us did well enough on our Spanish exams to test out of college language requirements), but mainly he was a character. If we misbehaved in class, he would glare down on us—lifting up on tiptoe to clear his five-foot-two frame over the podium—and say, "You can only get away with this because you're young, with fresh skins and bright eyes and shiny hair. If you were little old ladies, no one would let you behave this way." (Advanced Spanish, for some reason, consisted entirely of girls, though the school as a whole was evenly coed.) On boring days he would get us through the hour by performing flamenco dances at the front of the classroom; he had, he implied, been a flamenco dancer at one time. Once he took a group of us into San Francisco by train for an evening of Basque food and flamenco dancing. "Look!" he said excitedly as we came out onto the streets of North Beach at 10:30 P.M. "Lights! People! Real city life!" This was in marked contrast to downtown Palo Alto, which closed up at about 8:00, and near which Mr. Gamez had a two-room apartment, decorated completely in hot pink, on the upper floor of a condemned building. He had almost no expenses—he took the bus instead of owning a car, a virtually unheard-of economy among the employed in Palo Alto—and invested all his extra income in Mexican real estate.

For some reason I have no fond memories of secondary-school female teachers. Whether this is due to the selection process of the Palo Alto school system, or to that of my own memory, I can't say. But after the maternal warmth of my first-grade teacher, Mrs. Robinson, there is only a bleak expanse inhabited by the likes of Mrs. Sullivan, a music, French, and self-proclaimed elocution teacher whose iron-gray pompadour formed a stern cliff face abutting her forehead: she made us memorize John Masefield's "I Must Go Down to the Seas Again," taught us saccharine songs from *The Sound of Music*, and had a habit of gripping you so hard by the shoulder that her talons seemed to leave permanent marks. Or Mrs. French, who incompetently taught us "homemaking," boasted of her hand-sewn Hong Kong buttonholes, and insisted that Audrey Hepburn and Jackie Kennedy were only beautiful through the proper application of makeup and hairgrooming, while Elizabeth Taylor, though naturally beautiful, suffered from insuperable flaws of character. Or Mrs. McGilvray, who dragged us through an entire year of Western Civilization classes by reading aloud for the whole class period from Will and Ariel Durant, so that if you knew older students who'd taken the course the year before, or even five years before, you could just borrow their notes and daydream. Or the English teacher—her name is lost deep in my subconscious, and even her face has now faded away—who one day snatched me out of a group walking down the slick "redtop" corridor of Wilbur Junior High, pinned me against the green stucco walls, and hissed, "Why do you hate me? Tell me, why *do* you?" Or Miss Hurst, whose dislike of me and of calculus was so severe that, though I did well in high school math contests (even scoring higher on one exam than Larry Kells, the nasal-voiced school genius), I never took another math course after hers. Or ... but why go on? We've all had bad teachers. It's one of the expected, essential elements of education, as I tried to tell myself (with no consoling effect) when my eleven-year-old son ran up against one of these petty monsters a couple of years ago.

———

I never took a course from Mr. Jones myself, but I couldn't help being aware of his presence at Cubberley

High School. For a few years he actually succeeded in changing the way the school was run.

Ron Jones must have been fresh out of an education credential program when he first came to Cubberley—must have been, in other words, about twenty years younger than I am now. He had a blondish crewcut (an exception in those days of shaggy liberalism), intense, darting eyes, and a face that was simultaneously flat and mobile. If he hadn't been a radical young teacher, he could easily have passed for a junior officer in the army or a recent graduate of a police academy. He was so fresh-faced that even we students, at fifteen, sixteen, and seventeen, thought of him as young. Some even called him Ron, though to most he remained Mr. Jones.

He soon became associated with the general air of disruption that was beginning to permeate our high school campus. This was in 1966 or 1967, after Watts and the Free Speech Movement but before the major demonstrations that shook college campuses across the country. Cubberley, perhaps because of its proximity to Stanford, Berkeley, and San Francisco State, felt the shock waves early. Kids gathered at recess to smoke dope in the corners of the playing fields. Attendance at sports rallies dwindled. Dress codes disappeared. David Harris—then merely the student president at Stanford, and not yet Joan Baez's husband or a jailed draft resister—came to speak to us about protesting the Vietnam War. (The administration insisted that we invite another speaker at another date to represent the opposite viewpoint. Somebody from Young Republicans duly appeared, but nobody went to hear him.)

Mr. Jones arrived in the midst of this and generated more of it. His history classes became famous for their unorthodox procedures. Students found wandering in the halls without the required passes inevitably announced they were on an errand for Mr. Jones. It got around that attendance at his history classes was voluntary—an incredible violation of high school discipline. However, the net effect of this strange rule was not a diminution in Mr. Jones's class size. On the contrary, students were cutting their other classes to attend his sessions (lectures is not the right word) on contemporary world history. People were falling out the doors, squeezing into standing-room-only positions, to absorb his irregular teaching.

One of his inventions, I recall, was a movement called The Third Wave, intended to educate his students about the crowd psychology of the Third Reich. For two weeks he required all his students to participate in a centrally controlled social structure wherein hazel-eyed people were considered a superior race. The society had its own hand gestures and salutes, its own official vocabulary, its own regulations of conduct. Two weeks can be a long time in high school, and adolescents are by nature fanatics, so The Third Wave rose quickly and powerfully. At the end of the second week, Mr. Jones—terrified by the

fanatical obedience he had spawned, yet triumphant at
the success of his pedagogical experiment—called a halt
to the game. But the kids objected: they loved it; this
was a society whose rules they could understand; they
wanted to continue following their blond-haired, hazel-
eyed, idealistic leader. It was only through the most
strenuous and lengthy discussions that Mr. Jones at last
convinced his students they'd been led into a trap.

I only heard about The Third Wave, but I was directly
involved in another of Mr. Jones's inventions, known as
Idea Forum, or IF for short. Mr. Jones came up with the
idea that every Wednesday afternoon all normal classroom activities on the entire campus should cease. (One
can begin to discern a pattern, I now perceive, to his educational theories, but at the time each idea seemed new
and separate.) In place of regular classes we would have
a wide array of elective activities and seminars offered
by students and faculty alike. There would be no set
length—each session could occupy as much time as
it required—and students would be allowed to wander
from one event to another. The only rule would be that
you couldn't leave campus. A schedule published each
week would detail the various offerings, from seminars
on Bob Dylan's lyrics to discussions of German philosophy to ceramics workshops and improvisational dance
classes.

Somehow, with the support of numerous students behind him, Mr. Jones persuaded the administration to

allow this experiment. It must have been a bureaucratic nightmare: all regular classes had to be reduced to twenty-five-minute sessions in the morning to free up the afternoon, and rooms had to be found each week for a variable number of IF seminars, each running on its own schedule. Still, they gave it a try. "Perhaps if this one fails," the greyer heads may have murmured to each other, "Jones will give up his nonsense." Or maybe they were merely humoring him, stringing him along until they could find some official reason to oust him. In any case, IF lasted for about four weeks and then fizzled out without much opposition. Attendance was good, and people didn't leave campus; the question was whether they were learning anything.

Now that I am sometimes a teacher myself, I lean toward a rather authoritarian mode: lecturer standing in front of the classroom, guiding student participation with a heavy hand, disseminating opinions and information from a position of assuredly greater knowledge. (The students who like me may view this description as exaggerated self-parody; my detractors will insist I haven't gone far enough.) I scorn alternative methodologies and revisionist canons and anything that smacks of Sixties technique; I believe in teaching literature, or anything else, directly and analytically, and I don't think the subject matter should be limited to things the students can "identify" with.

But I only teach very occasionally, and that's the

closest I ever come to holding down a job. The rest of my life is composed like a series of Idea Forums: oddly segmented episodes pieced together throughout the day that contribute to one activity or another, bringing in some income or using up some energy, producing a short piece of writing or contributing to a long-term project, usually on my own but sometimes with a small group of people. I have almost always been self-employed; I am what the high school psychologists might have labeled "self-motivating." Did Mr. Jones's Idea Forum determine my whole life? Probably not. Most likely I would have turned out like this anyway. Still, I remember what I learned in those Idea Forum sessions far more clearly than I can recall any details of junior-year English or senior History. Among other things, I learned in a drama workshop that I am far too self-conscious ever to be an actor; I heard phrases like "existentialism" and "categorical imperative" for the first time; and I read, for the first *and* last time, sections of William Burroughs's *Naked Lunch.*

But what taught me even more was Mr. Jones's dismissal from Cubberley, which occurred the year after I graduated. Whether he was actually fired, or simply let go at the time of tenure review, remains shrouded in doubt in my under-informed memory. What I do know is that his departure had something to do with IF, The Third Wave, and all the other unusual things that took place under his supervision.

Ron Jones landed on his feet: he got a job teaching at the San Francisco Recreation Center for the Handicapped (where, to the best of my knowledge, he still works), took up small-press publishing, and even wrote and published a few mildly successful books of his own, including an account—far more detailed and accurate than mine—of the Third Wave experiment. Cubberley Senior High School, on the other hand, was shut down about fifteen years ago when the shrinkage of Palo Alto's student population made its continued maintenance economically infeasible. Such are the ironies, I suppose, through which the just eventually triumph over the unjust. But to the students who attended Cubberley during Mr. Jones's era, the irony we were left with is quite another one: the one inherent in the fact that even the "best" school districts, when their backs are against the wall, will inevitably choose order over imagination. I am fond of order myself: my ways of thinking about art, about work, about friendship, are all premised on a combination of order and something that is not order. But orderliness is a good servant and a poor master. Order needs to be kept in its place, lorded over by wilder and more eccentric forces, mocked and even abandoned occasionally. Only under those circumstances can it remain satisfying and useful rather than imprisoning. Or so I learned from Mr. Jones, nearly thirty years ago. It is one of the few things from my high school education that has endured—that, and a little bit of Spanish.

THINKING BACK ON HARVARD

A s a freshman I was assigned to a dormitory called Eliot Hall, which sounded to my Western ears like the name of the sort of person who would go to Harvard. Actually, it was one of the smaller, nicer, older buildings surrounding the Radcliffe Quad, and I was lucky to be among the ten or twelve incoming women who were housed there. The others included a Hyannisport Kennedy, a French Rothschild, and Benazir Bhutto, known to us all as Pinkie, who was eventually to become the first—and, to date, the only—female prime minister of Pakistan.

I had never even met a debutante before I went east to college, but Pinkie made the run-of-the-mill Radcliffe debutantes seem coarse and ordinary by comparison. The soles of her feet were as smooth and unblemished as the palms of most other girls' hands, for she had never in her life set foot outdoors without shoes on. Nor had she ever lifted the receiver of a ringing telephone before she came to Harvard; there had always been servants to answer the phone in Karachi. Her father, at the time she started college, was the foreign minister of Pakistan, and she already suspected that he might one day be president. What she did not suspect (how could she?) was that after his presidency he would be hanged by his political enemies.

Pinkie and I soon became known as the dormitory's champion loafers. We would lounge day and night in the centrally located living room of Eliot Hall, luring by-passers into our twenty-four-hour party of games and conversation. Pinkie taught me how to make batiks, and I in turn taught her to bake cakes from Betty Crocker mixes; she was so thrilled with this culinary accomplishment that she insisted on repeating it once or twice a week, with the result that we each gained about fifteen pounds during our first semester.

At the time, and for years afterward, I thought of Pinkie as a version of Shakespeare's Cleopatra. (She herself, at sixteen, was fond of quoting Enobarbus's description of the Egyptian queen, and I can still hear in my mind's ear the imperious, self-mocking inflection she gave to the line "Age cannot wither her, nor custom stale her infinite variety.") But now I realize that the Shakespearean character she most reminds me of is Prince Hal. For a long time she appeared to do nothing but play: having fun was her specialty, and she was good at it. When she first got to Harvard she seemed innocently giggly and high-spirited; in later years she developed a brassily ditzy, bubble-brained, Bright-Young-Things manner, as if the impulse to enjoy life had hardened into a mask. And then, long after I had ceased to see her, she all at once dropped the mask and became a serious, wily politician, her father's rightful heir. The change *seemed* sudden; yet if you had asked me, even as a freshman, to guess who among my acquaintance would eventually become a world-famous political figure, I would not have hesitated to answer, "Pinkie Bhutto."

———

In my time out from playing Falstaff to Pinkie's Hal, I became involved in curriculum reform. Why a seventeen-year-old from California believed herself qualified to tell a three-hundred-year-old institution what it should be teaching its students is not a question we need go into here. Suffice it to say that I threw myself into the effort with zeal. The major target of my opprobrium was Harvard's General Education requirement, which furthered the school's liberal arts principles by making the students take "Gen Ed" courses in science, social science, and the humanities. I can no longer reconstruct why I was so much against this; my argument had something to do with the admitted amateurism of the special courses, and something else to do with the restricted choice. My objection was certainly not based on my own Gen Ed experience, which was entirely positive: the geology course I had selected—taught by a very young associate professor named Stephen Jay Gould— was so good that I voluntarily enrolled in an additional semester of geology, even though I have never been able to tell one rock from another. ("Wendy! Stop hacking away at those garnets!" are the only words I can recall Stephen Jay Gould addressing to me, though I'm sure we must have had other conversations.)

Whatever my reasons, I was determined to wean Harvard from its ill-conceived pedagogical plan. I joined a group of undergraduate curriculum agitators, and we got ourselves put on the agenda of a Harvard faculty meeting, which was held in Sanders Theater, inside the appealingly monstrous old Memorial Hall. As one of our group's designated speakers, I was given three minutes to present my case. I can still recall the feeling of standing at the base of that huge bowl, with the semicircular rows of seats ranged in front of me, the lectern light shining on my pages, and my voice quavering out into the room. I had just reached the beginning of my last paragraph when I heard Nathan Pusey, the president of Harvard, announce from somewhere off to my left: "Time!" I read aloud my next sentence. "Time's up!" he barked again. At this I turned my head toward him and said, in a tone of voice that was slightly harsh and clearly audible throughout the theater, "Please let me finish!" Which he did, possibly because he was too surprised to do anything else. For years afterward, when I met faculty members, they would tell me they recognized me: I was the freshman who had told President Pusey to shut up. This perhaps makes me sound more rebellious than I was. It was a generally rebellious time, and I was more law-abiding than many; I believed, for instance, that orderly, legal processes could bring about the desired changes. (To a certain extent I still believe that—or rather, I believe that change which does *not* come about through orderly, legal processes is not the kind of change I want to experience.) This is not to say that I did not take advantage of the pervading chaos. When a student strike in the spring of 1970 enabled us to skip our exams and get "incompletes" if we chose, I happily took the easy way out in all my courses. But in strike meetings and planning sessions for antiwar demonstrations I usually found myself battling the extremists, those hardliners who answered all attempts to distinguish between subtly but crucially different positions with the comment "That's just a semantic issue." Once I ended up in a large roomful of these people, all shouting to be heard over each other's angry statements. I raised my hand. "Excuse me, can we have Robert's Rules of Order here?" I asked.

"Robert's Rules of *Order*," shrieked one of the angriest, "when babies are being *burned* in Vietnam?" All eyes turned toward me—condemningly, I thought—and I said nothing for the rest of the meeting.

———

By the time I was a junior, political activity on campus had pretty much died down, and I had moved from the isolated precincts of Radcliffe to the more centrally located Dunster House, at Harvard. These distinctions between "Harvard" and "Radcliffe" would make no sense at all to a student attending the university now: they are all Harvard students, male and female alike, and they all start out in the freshman dorms in Harvard Yard. But when I started college in 1969, Radcliffe was essentially an old-fashioned women's school, with strictly enforced curfews, special telephone etiquette for dealing with male callers, and Saturday night milk-and-cookies served to those girls unfortunate enough not to be out on dates. This all came as rather a shock to me, since I had assumed Harvard and Radcliffe were completely coed. I hadn't realized that only the classes were mixed. (But then, what did I know about Radcliffe? No one of my acquaintance had ever gone there; I only applied because I had read about it in Helen Keller's autobiography.) Luckily, reality caught up with my expectations in the spring of 1970, when a few hardy pioneers from Harvard moved into the Radcliffe dorms and vice versa. By 1971, when I moved down to Dunster House, coeducation was in full swing.

I soon fell into a comfortable pattern which was to last

for most of my final two years at Harvard. A habitually early riser, I would be in the Dunster dining room at the start of breakfast—say, 7:30 or 8:00—and would stay there for roughly an hour and a half, chatting with a gradually expanding group of my friends. Then I'd go back to my rooms (my "suite," as it was rather pretentiously called) and read until lunch, at which I would spend a full two hours talking with an even larger gathering. Ditto for dinner. In between I might have an afternoon seminar which required me to go out, but I tried to keep these academic engagements down to two or at most three days a week. I almost never took a morning lecture course—partly because that would have required me to leave home before lunch, and partly because lecture courses entailed exams, which were much less controllable than papers. A seminar paper, I had discovered, could be completed in four days: two days to do the reading and research, one day to write, one day to type. (I used an old pale-blue Hermes portable, which is still taking up space in my basement though I haven't touched the keys in decades.) This meant that Reading Period—that sixteen-day stretch of time between the end of classes and the beginning of exams—could be used to complete the work for all four of my courses. And this, in turn, meant that I did no work to speak of during the rest of the semester. Instead, I talked. My memory of college is of one long, intermittently interrupted conversation.

It sounds fun, but in fact we were all pretty miserable. Alumni would show up at times and announce that their Harvard years had been the best of their lives. "Jeez!" we said to each other. "If these are the best years of our lives, I hate to think what comes next!" Some people got so depressed they had breakdowns; the rest of us just muddled through, staying up half the night, drinking, lying around, and endlessly talking. This tedious but addictive routine would be punctuated by an occasional Early Music concert in the Dunster House Library (I particularly remember the golden quality of the late-afternoon light as it came through the tall windows and shone on the library's mellow woodwork, an exact visual counterpart of the rich Bach or Corelli chords we were listening to at the time) or an even more occasional stage performance by Dunster House's resident theater fanatics (including Christopher Durang, who wrote our Christmas pageant, and Al Franken, who starred in it as Saint John the Baptist). But these breaks in the routine were relatively rare. Most of us were content to do nothing day after day.

To the general sources of depression that afflicted us all, I added a special one of my own: the cold. I had gone east to college in part to become adapted to all sorts of weather. As a teenager I scorned the California softness, the paradise weather, those countless days of sun marked off by a relatively brief season of rain. I longed to be in a real climate, where I could undergo the sort of weather I had read about in books. But what I discovered at Harvard was that I could not tolerate the bone-chilling cold of a Massachusetts winter. It made me want to curl up and hibernate, and to a certain extent that's what I was doing.

———

One day, on one of my rare visits to Widener Library, I was standing on line waiting to check out a book when I happened to glance down at the library card of the man standing next to me. I had already noticed its owner: he was an elderly man with a prominent nose and sharp, hooded eyes, and he made me think of an eagle. Idly, I read the name printed on his card. Then, without pausing to consider, I turned to him and said, "Lewis Mumford! *You're* Lewis Mumford! I've admired your work for years—*The City in History* is one of my favorite books!" He seemed pleased, and invited me back to Leverett House (where he was a visiting something-or-other) to have tea and meet his wife, Sophie.

This, I suppose, was a turning point, because Lewis Mumford told me about Patrick Geddes, the Scottish city planner about whom I ended up writing my undergraduate thesis. And in order to write the thesis I spent a summer in Edinburgh doing research. (Some generous grantmaking body at Harvard paid for the trip, but I'm afraid I no longer remember the philanthropy's name.) And while I was in Britain I went to visit a former professor of mine, a man who had spent one semester teaching Victorian literature at Harvard but was now back at his usual post at Bristol.

"What are you going to do with yourself after you graduate?" said Christopher Ricks. We were on a lengthy walk through the streets of Bristol; Christopher walked very fast (he still does, a quarter-century later) and I was struggling to keep up.

"Oh, I guess I'll just go to law school," I panted.

"Are you particularly interested in the law?"

"No, not at all. But it seems the easiest thing to do next."

"Have you ever thought of going to graduate school in English?"

"I've thought of it," I said, "but every time I'm in a roomful of academics, I can't picture myself turning out like that."

"Can you picture yourself turning out like a roomful of lawyers?" he countered. He had me stumped, as my silence admitted.

Then he tried another approach. "Sometimes, if we have talents we choose not to explore—out of fear, or social distaste, or for some other reason—it's like leaving a room in a house closed off for years. It gets stuffy in there. Sometimes you need to open the door." (Most likely these are not his exact words; all I remember is the metaphor itself, which struck me vividly.) "And if you don't like the idea of graduate school in America, you could always try Oxford or Cambridge. They accept Americans for special degrees, and it might give you a chance to see whether you want to go on in English literature, without the same career pressure you'd find in a Harvard or Yale Ph.D. program."

A month later, I filed my application to Cambridge University. And a year after that, in the fall of 1973, I found myself at King's College, Cambridge.

AN AMERICAN IN ENGLAND

F rom the time it was founded in 1441 to the Michaelmas term of the year before I arrived, some five hundred years later, King's College was open only to male students. Women had been admitted to Cambridge starting in 1869, but they were confined to the three women's colleges and only shared university-wide lecture courses with the men. As at Harvard, all the real action—including much of the teaching—took place at the residential-college level, so it was very lucky for me that in 1972 King's and two other centrally located Cambridge colleges decided to break the Oxbridge tradition by admitting women.

I was aware of my luck, but I tended to think of it along broader lines than those of gender. I had escaped everything—the shallow newness of California, the cold insularity of Harvard, the ugly situation in American politics (which at that historical moment combined Richard Nixon and the Vietnam War), my family, my friends, the

question of what to do with my life—and had leapt into
an entirely new dimension. England was, for me, a dream:
a place where bus conductors read Wilfred Owen's poetry while they were on their breaks (I knew this because
I had peeked at the book cover while waiting for the bus
to bring me from the train station to King's); where a
humanely socialist political party was a mass organization rather than a wild-eyed fringe group; where courtesy in public behavior was the rule rather than the
exception; and where astonishingly beautiful buildings
and grounds were inhabited by the likes of me. Harvard
had been a place of privilege, but it was nonetheless run
as a large bureaucracy, with official channels and impersonal procedures and unavoidable delays, whereas Cambridge was run like a private club. Once my check from
America was late in coming; I simply went to see the Bur-
sar of King's College (a large, kindly South African Jew)
and he lent me fifty pounds to tide me over. Another time
I went to him to urge the College's involvement in building low-cost housing for town residents, and he wrote
out a thousand-pound check on the spot. That's how
things were done in the Cambridge of that time, and the
sense of ease both thrilled and moved me.

Even now, the assertion of one's collegiate privileges
is a remarkably easy, gentlemanly affair. Recently, when
I was in Cambridge for a conference at Downing College,
I walked over to King's College to take a look at my old

haunts. I was dressed in jeans and a T-shirt, and the gowned don standing at the college gate looked as if he were about to tell me that the grounds were closed to tourists for the day. "I was, or am, a—" I began, and before I had even reached the phrase "member of King's College," he was waving me through the gate. Tickled at my success, I decided to test how far my realm extended. Queen's College, the lovely old Tudor-brick complex next door to King's, was charging a pound per head to tour the buildings. "I'm a member of King's," I announced, and was instantly admitted free. The scam could be worked infinitely.

Most of the Englishmen I know now (they tend to be men rather than women) have a passion for things American. Our movies, our literature, our political movements, our cities, our pop music, our television shows: they are all considered vastly better and more exciting than the tiny, tidy, overly cautious British version of same. But when I first lived there in the early Seventies, this was all reversed. America was a rather despicable place to be from. Our greatest shame was the Vietnam War, but there were other national outrages: the relatively recent assassinations of John F. Kennedy, Robert Kennedy, and Martin Luther King Jr.; the racial and economic inequities that had led to the Watts riots; the incredible shenanigans exhibited in the Watergate hearings; and the federally approved firebombing of the Symbionese

Liberation Army headquarters (that era's equivalent of the Waco disaster), which took place live on American television while I was at Cambridge and shocked my English friends to the core. England may have been a deeply class-ridden society—it *was*, and still is, a deeply class-ridden society—but even its political conservatives, when I lived there, espoused views that would have been considered left-wing by American standards. Universally subsidized medical care, free higher education, guaranteed unemployment payments for life, nationally owned railways and utilities were all deemed normal and natural. Public space was considered more important than private space, so that parks, art museums, and the London Underground were beautifully kept up, whereas most middle-class people survived without central heating, modern kitchen appliances, or fully effective plumbing. At the time this seemed to me an admirable way to live.

Academically, too, Cambridge fit my requirements perfectly. The standard course of education there consisted of a series of "supervisions"—weekly one-on-one meetings between a student and a college faculty member—supplemented, as desired, by lectures given at the university's departmental buildings. In some fields, such as chemistry or applied mathematics, you skipped lectures at your peril, but in English they were entirely optional: all the work for the final exams—the "Tripos"—

was done in supervisions. This suited me fine. I occa-sionally tried attending some lectures, but in each case I gave up well before the end of term. Meanwhile I was scouring the university for the best supervisors, ranging beyond King's to the precincts of Gonville and Caius, Clare, and the other colleges. As the result of this entre-preneurship (no one but an American, it was implied, would actually *seek out* a supervisor), I received an in-comparable literary education during those years.

For "practical criticism"—the Cambridge-identified close-reading method invented by I. A. Richards and fruitfully elaborated by William Empson—I studied with the kindly Joan Bennett, an expert in the meta-physical poets, as well as with the eccentrically brilliant Jeremy Prynne, a poet so avant-garde that his work was generally acknowledged to be unreadable. (Prynne's col-lege rooms were lined with rare books of a kind I had never seen before, such as a folio-sized vellum-bound edition of Dr. Johnson's Dictionary; only at Cambridge, I decided, could the literary avant-garde be so luxuri-ously traditional.) For "moralists"—a philosophy-based course that ran from Aristotle to Freud—I engaged in weekly arguments with John Casey, a politically conser-vative don who dressed in flowing velvet robes, refused to tutor women students (he made an exception in my case, possibly as a favor to Christopher Ricks), and treated my pipsqueak ideas with the utmost intellectual respect. And for "tragedy"—a required Tripos exam that took in dramatists from Aeschylus to Beckett—I had Wilbur Saunders, a forceful, forthright Australian whose lectures in Shakespeare and Jane Austen I had admiringly (if briefly) attended. After my first few weeks of studying with Saunders, he gently told me that I wrote too much like a Harvard student, relying on unwieldy, impersonally deployed Latinate phrases that didn't really mean anything. I was cut to the quick, and I went back to my room in Peas Hill Hostel to sulk. Then I began to work on my weekly essay in the manner he had suggested to me. I used short, simple sentences that expressed exactly what I felt and no more: "I don't always think Socrates is fair. I don't like the way he treats Antigone . . ." etc. From there, over the course of the year, I built up my paragraphs from scratch. To the extent that I have one, I owe my critical-prose style in large part to Will Saunders, and I am grateful to him, wherever he may be.

This intellectual development had its parallel in my emotional development: that is, in both instances I had to lose myself in order to find another, more workable version of myself. I know of no American who attended Cambridge in those years who did *not* have some kind of breakdown, and I was no exception. In my case, and I imagine in the case of many others, the dreamlike ease of the place was partly responsible. (It was aided, no doubt, by the quiet boredom, the dank weather, and the depressingly pervasive, unruffled respectability.) Because I had escaped reality, I was free to crack up. England, or at least Cambridge, seemed to hold a kind of safety net beneath me that had not been there in America; no permanent harm could possibly come to me in this idyllic setting, this fictional place. And so I let go.

During my first year I had fallen in love with a fellow King's student, a working-class, London-born, Grantham-bred chemistry graduate named Shaun. We met at King's, but we got to know each other mainly through our involvement in Labour Party politics. (Not only did I join the British Labour Party during my first term at Cambridge—I was also an elected student representative to the party's local governing body. People seemed remarkably unconcerned about the presence of an "outside agitator," and in all the months of canvassing I did before the 1974 General Elections, no one ever questioned me about my American accent; perhaps they just thought I came from a part of Britain they hadn't yet visited.)

Shaun and I began as friends but soon fell into a love affair. The consequences were so dire that I have never again made the same mistake. My relationship with Shaun was clearly meant to be a friendship (it still *is* a friendship, twenty-five years later—we were able to patch things up once the dust had cleared), but I, or he, or both of us had insisted on turning it into something else. We had about twelve months of a horrible relationship and then we broke up, after which we continued to have an even more horrible relationship, of a hardly less connected type, until I finally left England. Each of us felt captivated, victimized, and ultimately destroyed by the other, but because I was a woman, and American, I was more vocal and expressive about my distress. Shaun just became silent and angry.

I had had unhappy love affairs at Harvard (it was impossible to get through college in those days without them, and probably the same is true now), but nothing in my past could compare with the sense of annihilation I felt during my battle with Shaun. I remember thinking: When I am alone in a room, it is as if there is no one here. I had allowed him to become identified in my mind with the England I loved, and I had then imagined myself to be a new person inhabiting that wonderful country. When the love affair ended, the country turned darkly unfriendly and its new inhabitant disintegrated, leaving me homeless and—I was going to say solitary, but that implies the presence of one, whereas I felt nonexistent. I deduced from my reading that this was not an uncommon experience, but the reading didn't help me feel any better, since I identified with all the most depressing people: Miriam in *Sons and Lovers*, Miss Havisham in *Great Expectations*. Just as, when you are having an illicit affair, all great literature seems to be about adultery, so it seemed to me then that all the best novels were about broken hearts. In the midst of this disaster, around Christmas of my second year, my mother arrived in London for a visit. My sister was already in England at the time, on a year's break from college, but since she too was coping with an unhappy love affair, her presence had been of minimal comfort—and in any case I was in Cambridge and she was at least two hours away, in Hampstead. The three of us gathered at my sister's bedsitter. I had not foreseen how I would feel at this familial encounter. (My sister, who by now has several degrees in matters relating to mental health, always points out to me that I *never* foresee how I will feel in such situations, with the consequence that I am always unpleasantly surprised. She herself finds it best to be prepared for the worst at all times, and as a result of her pessimism she is able to be comparatively sanguine in the face of disaster when, as expected, it arrives.) What I felt, as it turned out, was tremendous anger at my mother for divorcing my father. I believed, with an insistent logic and a complete lack of humane reasonableness, that this single act of hers sixteen years earlier had led directly, step by inevitable step, to my current unhappiness with Shaun. My first response to this feeling was to remain stonily, excessively silent. (Possibly, it now occurs to me, I was unconsciously imitating Shaun's behavior toward me.) My mother perceived that I was in trouble and she clearly wanted to do something, but I think she was afraid *of* me as well as *for* me. Finally, however, she asked me what was wrong, at which point I launched into a diatribe, reduced her to tears, and stormed back to Cambridge on the first available train.

That was the low point. Shortly thereafter I began seeing a psychologist—an extremely intelligent and ultimately helpful woman, the wife of a Cambridge anthropology professor. I also developed little routines to get me through the day. I made lists of people who depressed me and people who cheered me up (Shaun was on neither, since it still gave me a charge to see him even though it also made me unhappy), and I tried to associate only with the latter. Eventually I even had another love affair or two—small, harmless episodes that didn't touch me deeply.

I also decided to go back to America. I had been told I could get a place doing research at Cambridge, and a part of me very much wanted to stay in England forever. But a saner and, luckily, stronger part knew I had to get out of there. The English people of my acquaintance all considered California the only place in America worth living in, and I had been getting the same message from the books I was reading by Aldous Huxley and Christopher Isherwood. So being in England, oddly enough, made it possible for me to think about going back to California in a way that being at Harvard never had.

I applied to Berkeley's Ph.D. program in English. I wasn't sure what I would do when I got there—whether I would finish the degree or not, whether I would ever want to teach, how I would go about supporting myself for all those years of graduate school—but it seemed as good a way as any to get out of the mess I was in at the moment. As always happens in such cases, the very act of trying to get out of the mess, the exertion of will on my own behalf, went a long way toward making me feel better. And this, in turn, enabled me to begin looking outward at the world again, instead of just inward at my own unhappiness.

CONSULTANTS

F or the first few months of our consulting careers, my business partner and I couldn't get over the feeling that no one would ever hire us. And why should they? Katharine and I were both graduate students in English at UC Berkeley, and, strictly speaking, we knew nothing about the areas in which we were seeking employment. All we had to recommend us were our Ivy League and Oxbridge degrees, which were prominently cited on our business brochure. In fact, our brochure consisted almost entirely of our educational résumés, since at that point we had nothing else to advertise. Our implicit motto was: If you can write, you can think; and if you can think, you can do public policy consulting. There may have been a flaw somewhere in this logical train. Or the problem may just have been our clothes. (We hadn't discovered Dress for Success.) At any rate, no one hired us at the beginning.

Every few days, or as often as our morale could stand

it, we'd pile into my beat-up old Volkswagen and drive down to the Peninsula looking for work. It was summer (the summer of 1977, to be exact), and my car had no air conditioning; on the contrary, it had a broken heater that wouldn't shut off. To make matters worse, our only decent skirts were winter wool. Sweaty and rumpled, we would emerge from the car in some place like Redwood City, or Cupertino, or Mountain View, and march unannounced into the office of the chief city planning official. There we would try to talk him (it was always a him) into hiring us for cost-benefit studies, housing plans, growth analyses—anything, in short, that his office had money for, or happened to be doing. He would listen politely, accept our brochure, and show us out.

I don't know why we chose the Peninsula as our hunting ground. Perhaps we felt that the East Bay (where we lived) and San Francisco (where most consultants worked) were too poor to have the excess cash to waste on us. The Peninsula, that stretch of luxuriant suburban development extending south of San Francisco along the west side of the bay, seemed ripe for sacking. I had grown up on the Peninsula, and Katharine had hardly ever been there before. We both hated it, with an equal but opposite force. To her New England sensibility it represented all that was worst about California: squeaky-clean newness, shopping malls as cultural centers, tawdry highway-side development, and city halls that, in architectural terms, could just as well have been high school administration buildings or dentists' offices. For me it was the giant maw of childhood, threatening to snatch me up from the realm of hard-won adulthood (my own *car!* a *business brochure!*) and swallow me whole.

We were briefly rescued from this series of futile trips by a job secured for us by Katharine's brother. A contact of a friend of his, or a friend of a contact (these things are hard to differentiate in the world of big business), was working or had been working for the B. Dalton bookstore chain, which was about to open a large outpost on Fifth Avenue in Manhattan. Some ambitious interior designer had envisioned a "bas-relief" (that was the exact phrase we were given) consisting of literary names, places, and titles, to be encoded in enduring plaster of Paris, just inside the main front window on a wall visible from the street. Katharine and I—or rather, our firm— won the august task of coming up with the names. We were to submit four lists: Fifty Great Authors, Fifty Great Books, Fifty Great Literary Characters, and Fifty Great Literary Places. We had quite a good time coming up with the items (I was particularly proud of Café Deux Magots and the House of Usher), and engaged in spirited arguments over "merit" versus "representation" (for example, could we list three Shakespeare plays and two Faulkner novels if we didn't include anything by Ben Jonson or Hemingway?). For years afterward, on my occasional trips to New York, I would stroll down that block of Fifth Avenue merely to witness our triumph—a triumph only slightly marred by the fact that the B. Dalton people had thrown out some of our most carefully selected choices to make room for the likes of Scarlett O'Hara and the Valley of the Dolls.

This amusing task, unfortunately, only took us about two and a half hours (already wily in the ways of consulting, we billed, I believe, for three), and we were soon out on the road again. We did eventually come up with one employer through the Drop-In Assault Technique: a place called Far West Laboratory for Educational Research. (You can tell by the name that they *would* hire someone off the street.) And in the long run we even managed to pile up a substantial list of clients, including the U.S. Department of Housing and Urban Development, the Alameda County Legal Aid Society, the San Francisco Department of Social Services, and the United Farm Workers.

We called ourselves Lesser & Ogden Associates. Katharine's boyfriend called us the Rip-Off Sisters. This is not to say that we were bad consultants. I think we were probably among the more honest, useful (and certainly cheap) members of the consulting trade during the years that I have subsequently come to think of as the Golden Brown era—that bountiful period when Jerry Brown's governorship, sandwiched between those of

Reagan and Deukmejian, overlapped with Jimmy Carter's presidency to produce (in California, at least) a rich panoply of social services. Such services are the carrion on which "good" consultants feed. Too pure to sully ourselves with business dealings as such, we circled instead around the moribund carcass of America's concern for its own poor. My partner and I wanted to help people, however indirectly; we also wanted to make a living. Our backgrounds in English literature ensured that "indirectly" would be the operative word, since our only access to the social services lay through the manipulation of language.

Unfortunately, it was a form of language that, in its degradation, effectively counteracted any good intentions we may have had. For what the language of public policy and social service consulting does is to eliminate the human factor. "Planning is something you do to other ·people," cracked a city planner at the firm where I did my high school apprenticeship; he seemed confident that he, at least, would never be redeveloped out of a home. But the situation is even more dire than that. Planning (in which I include all large-scale public policy activities) is a nearly autonomous process which supersedes both planner and plannee. Like the ferocious machine in Chaplin's *Modern Times*, it threatens to consume even the individual at its helm.

My partner and I were essentially hired guns. The fact

that the agencies which hired us were the good guys in the "war on poverty" made some but surprisingly little difference. We were brought in to solve problems; we did our bit and departed. "A *problem*," Richard Ohmann astutely remarks in his book *English in America*, "is a chunk of reality distanced from the self and made objective. There it can be manipulated, and a solution found." We found solutions to the satisfaction of our employers, but whether our actions ever made the slightest difference to any "low-income populations" is something I seriously doubt.

The poor do not exist in the world of public policy consulting; they have been replaced entirely by "the low-income." Like all the other euphemisms which pepper the consulting trade, this one has its deleterious aspects. Poor people are distinct and disturbing. They ask you for money on the street, or show up in sad Christmas columns in the daily paper, or sit on the sidewalks with their meager belongings (and pets, and sometimes even children) spread out around them. They impinge on your sensibility. The low-income, in contrast, are a faceless mass of statistics, a portion of a government chart about annual family incomes. The word, moreover, has no inherent negative connotations: it could even be something good, like "low-cholesterol" or "low-cost." Ostensibly introduced to salvage the self-worth of the population it describes (since nobody in supposedly classless America would want to be categorized as "poor"), the term actually removes those it denotes from the arena of public concern. It somehow implies, with its thermometer-like objectivity, that their condition is merely due to a temporary drop in the collective economic temperature.

Money is a dirty word in the consulting business. Perhaps this is because the social planners don't want to be accused of "throwing money at a problem"; more likely, it is because there is so little money to throw. And the consultants themselves are not eager to be reminded that they are earning filthy lucre for their good deeds. So the standard requests for proposals (RFPs, in the professional lingo) never describe a consulting contract in terms of a bare amount of money; rather, the expected payment is expressed as "degree of support," which in turn boils down to "person-hours" or "person-days" (or even "person-months," in a really lucrative contract). And the social service agencies to which consultants consult do not spend money either: they have "budgetary requirements" and receive "funding."

To counteract this vagueness at the heart of their profession, consultants have seized in desperation on the language of the machinist. The part of a proposal which can be used over and over again for different clients (the part describing the consulting firm's capabilities and general problem-solving approach) is called the "boilerplate." The basics of an area of expertise are referred to as the "nuts and bolts." "Does he know the nuts and bolts of redevelopment?" one might ask about a potential new employee—not querying his ability to put up a steel-core highrise, but trying to find out if he knows how to get through the requisite government paperwork. In its futile attempt to force some kind of concreteness into inherently abstract pursuits, such language drains these mechanical terms of any real meaning. Consulting *is* mechanical, but only in the idiomatically metaphorical sense.

In addition to its person-hours, its boilerplate, and its nuts and bolts, every consulting document to which I was ever a party had to have its "Executive Summary." This appendage, which always came at the front of the document, consisted of two to ten pages recapitulating, in brief, the contents of the whole proposal or report. In other words, it was a plain old summary. What was "executive" about it? Rumor had it that the practice had begun during the gubernatorial reign of Ronald Reagan, when the state's chief executive professed himself unwilling or unable to read any document longer than ten pages. Whatever its origins, the Executive Summary had its practical uses: it gave a false air of efficiency and managerial adeptness to what might otherwise seem a morass of interminable verbiage. The opening remarks implied (without having to assert it outright, which would have entailed taking some responsibility) that there were executives in charge, people who knew how to execute things.

"No ideas but in things," William Carlos Williams strenuously advocated. The entire history of the consulting profession might be viewed as an attempt to give the lie to that poetic dictum. "No ideas but in other ideas," or, more accurately, "No ideas but in meaningless abstractions," is the implicit battle cry of the consultant. Even the professions that ostensibly deal in tangibles— the urban planners, the housing experts—linguistically reach for intangibility. Once I was interviewed for a subcontract position by a man who produced environmental impact reports, housing plans, and other pieces of paper connected with urban design. Casting a suspicious glance at my mainly literary educational résumé, he barked, "Come on, would you know a housing element if it hit you on the head?" I responded with a look of affronted self-justification. In truth, I had no idea what a housing element was; all I could be sure of was that it was *not* a house. My potential employer's bizarre turn of phrase left me with a haunting mental image: unlike the Wicked Witch of the East, who in *The Wizard of Oz* was actually squashed by a house, I was to be brained by a technically nonexistent, purely linguistic "housing element."

Sometimes a consultant's sleight of phrase is entirely purposeful, aimed at avoiding rejection, detection, or (at the very least) uncomfortable cross-examination. I'm convinced this was the case, for instance, in a project Lesser & Ogden Associates did for an eccentric little San Francisco organization. Consisting almost entirely of a battered but natty-looking ex-alcoholic and his female sidekick, this "organization" proposed to cure alcoholism through the heavy application of various vitamins and minerals (zinc, I remember, being chief among them). We were to write a proposal for the treatment center. Actually, the technique appeared to make some sense, and there were even a few medical reports to back it up. But our clients, wary of being written off as health-food faddists, forbade us to use the word "vitamins" in the proposal. We were to refer exclusively to their "orthomolecular" approach to alcoholism.

At other times, though, the euphemisms may be merely the unintentional linguistic cruelties habitually spawned by large bureaucracies. In one case Katharine and I were hired to create a "cost of living index for G.A. recipients" in Alameda County. This sounds pleasantly clean and statistical, with the distasteful truth safely hidden away in the usual alphabet soup. (Part of what distinguishes members of the consulting guild from outsiders, incidentally, is their pronunciation of acronyms and abbreviations. HUD—the Department of Housing and Urban Development—is always "Hud," like the Paul Newman movie, whereas General Assistance is "Gee A," not "Gah.") What the Alameda County job in fact entailed was coming up with a monthly sum on which the poorest of the welfare poor could survive by living in single-room-occupancy hotels, eating foods that fulfilled only the minimal nutritional requirements of the Department of Agriculture, and taking no more than one round-trip bus ride per day. The fact that we were doing this research for a good cause (to raise the minimum General Assistance payment from an excruciating $159 per month to an only slightly less unbearable $286 per month) hardly made us feel any better about the existence we were envisioning for the beneficiaries of our work. A "cost of living index" had, in this sense, no relationship to a life.

In carrying out the G.A. project we relied on a basic tool of the consulting trade, the specially tailored survey "instrument." The word, standard in all survey-using professions, suggests either fine tuning or delicate surgery; in either case the implication is one of subtle movements, regard for aesthetic form, and skilled elimination of pain. But the reality is just the opposite. A survey instrument is a blunt tool with which one bludgeons the frequently unwilling victim into virtual unconsciousness, at the same time numbing one's own sensibilities into a similar state. Even before the proliferation of computers, it was a device aimed at promoting dialogue between one machine and another. The only way a human being could effectively use it was to memorize the questions and then throw the damn thing away, hoping that all the salient points would somehow be raised in a normal conversation.

Katharine and I realized even at the height of our consulting careers that there was something drastically wrong, or at best ludicrous, about the language of our profession. To keep sane, we developed a series of private jokes and references that played off our sense of this ludicrousness. When we first started the firm, I remember, I was in the midst of reading *J.R.*, William Gaddis's marvelous and horrifyingly accurate rendering of corporate babble. One highly placed executive in the novel kept talking about "putting out brushfires" every time he had a minor crisis to handle. Lesser & Ogden Associates seized on this phrase, trotting it out gleefully whenever a snag presented itself. Part of our delight in the formulation lay in its utter inappropriateness—and therefore its ironically pleasing aptness—to the work of a consultant. Taken literally, the phrase suggests a band of resolute cowboys, ranchowners, and rural sheriffs joining together to stamp out a blaze that threatens homes and livestock. It has the romance of a western, the immediacy of flame. Consulting, of course, has neither. Yet on some level the consultant would like to think of himself as the modern equivalent of the old self-reliant dogooder, a kind of white-collar Wyatt Earp rushing out to right wrongs and then moving on to the next "problem." But the real problem is that there are no brushfires in the consulting business—no rectifiable emergencies, no burning realities, no urgent demands for action. It's all just smoke.

In retrospect, however, I have many reasons to be grateful for my brief public policy consulting career, which lasted from 1977 to about the end of 1980 or possibly the beginning of 1981 (the demise of our firm corresponding closely with the election and inauguration of President Reagan). For one thing, it enabled me to survive for more than three years without getting a real job, a lesson I absorbed so well that I have *yet* to hold down a forty-hour-a-week, benefits-paying, promotion-track position. More important, it taught me that what I needed from my work was a tangible product, something I could point to at the end of the day, or the year, or the lifetime, and say, "I did this." (It seems to have had pretty much the same effect on Katharine. After an interim job at Bay Area Rapid Transit, she went on to an unusual career in real estate development, including the construction of some incredibly beautiful stone-and-tile houses in the Umbrian countryside.) My first response to this realization was to found a little magazine, *The Threepenny Review*, whose preservable, complete-in-themselves quarterly issues were intended to provide the concrete proof of my labor—as indeed they have. But it would be ten years before the fledgling magazine could pay me any kind of salary, and in the meantime I had to support myself. With this crass motive in mind, I sold my services, at the beginning of the 1980s, to a wealthy Bay Area foundation in need of an "arts and environment" consultant.

STRANGE MEETING

―――――

I n 1981 I briefly served as the point of contact
between the Synanon drug rehab organization
and a group of ranchers in Marin County. As
I knew nothing about drugs and even less about ranching, I was perhaps not ideally suited to my role, but this
didn't seem to bother my employers at the foundation,
who had engineered the encounter between the two
parties.

Shortly before I appeared on the scene, the increasingly embattled Synanon, already famous for its unconventional (not to say bizarrely authoritarian) residential
treatment methods, had decided to move out of Marin
County to a less accessible location. This was just after
the *Point Reyes Light,* a tiny West Marin newspaper, had
won a Pulitzer Prize for exposing some of the creepier
aspects of the treatment program's operations. Synanon wanted to sell its 3,300 acres as quickly as possible; the locals feared this meant that prime agricultural

land would be lost forever to vulture-like developers. To avert the potential environmental disaster, the foundation bought the land itself, all the while planning to re-sell at least some of it to local ranchers. My job was supposedly to oversee the transition.

Synanon's holdings in West Marin consisted of three separate parcels: the Maggetti Ranch, the Walker Creek Ranch, and the Marconi Property. The last, a beautiful sixty-three-acre site facing out over Tomales Bay, was so named because in 1905 RCA had developed it as a radio research facility, apparently hoping to lure over Guglielmo Marconi, the then-famous inventor of the "wireless telegraph." But he never came, and something of that sense of wistful incompletion still lingered about the old inn and the outbuildings that occupied the gorgeous grounds. It was the type of place ideally suited to an artist colony, an Esalen-like therapy center, or a terminal disease hospital—the sort of place where the inner turmoil of the visitors would be both soothed by and absorbed into the ominously lush natural setting—and that was indeed the kind of use for which the foundation planned to reserve it. So the Marconi Property was not to be turned over immediately, and only the two ranches were up for possible sale.

This was complicated, however, by the fact that Synanon, or some remnant of it, was still occupying the ranch properties. How this essentially urban program got to the ranches in the first place was one of those typically fluky tales (typical of that period, I mean). The Synanon Foundation had begun as a drug rehab program in Los Angeles, where winos and heavy drug users would be taken in off the streets, cleaned up, and enabled to resume relatively normal lives. At one time—perhaps this is still true—Synanon held the record for getting people off drugs and preventing recidivism; it was by far the most effective program in the field. Somewhere along the line, though, it begin shifting from a rather curiously ideological drug treatment program (not that any of them *aren't* ideological—a strong and often eccentric moral stance seems to go with the territory) to what its detractors labeled a cult. Precisely what defines a cult has been the subject of much discussion in California, particularly since the Jonestown catastrophe, and I am not interested at the moment in placing Synanon in a carefully constructed definitional box. Suffice it to say that the group's founder, Charles Dederich, came more and more to view himself, and to be viewed by Synanon's members, as a father/king figure ruling over a self-contained society. This tendency increased with shocking rapidity after the death of Dederich's second wife, a well-liked woman who had reportedly been the moral and emotional center of the organization; and Dederich was eventually indicted on a number of criminal counts, amid a buzz of gossip that included stories of wild booze parties and indiscriminate sexual pairings. To this day many Californians who hear the word Synanon think first of a rattlesnake in a mailbox—an incident that may have been either a dastardly deed aimed at a Synanon "enemy" or a natural hazard of suburban life, depending on whose story you believe.

As Synanon grew more "ideological" and less "therapeutic" (for lack of a better pair of oppositions), it also came to appeal to a different class of customer. Instead of the helpless, poverty-stricken street addicts, it was now attracting professional people: lawyers, doctors, stockbrokers, and tax accountants who, with their wives and children, wanted to flee the drug-afflicted, crime-ridden urban environment for a secure, uncorrupted, isolated community. That and the chance to vent their psychological spleens in the highly charged Synanon encounter groups known as "Stews" seem to have been what brought in the upper middle classes. Synanon became a place to live permanently, not just a place to be treated. And, somewhat in the manner of an Israeli kibbutz, the nonprofit Synanon Foundation took over all the resources of its individual members, which had by now become considerable. These lifetime savings and proceeds from the sales of houses and cars, plus ongoing salaries from high-paying professional jobs, when added to the income from Synanon's "industries" (mail-order office supply sales and so forth, for which the resident "employees" were of course unpaid), gave Dederich and his fellow leaders quite a tidy sum to play with. It was at about this stage in its history, I think, that Synanon consolidated its entire operation by moving everything to West Marin.

Marin County is burdened with the image of affluent, spoiled, California-weirdo suburbia, an image which unfortunately rests on a sizable measure of truth. West Marin, however, is somewhat different. On the Pacific side of the coastal range that divides the county in half, civilization thins out, and its discontents are accordingly lessened. Towns are small and far apart; they are likely to contain only a single main drag with a post office, a grocery store, a variety store, and perhaps a coffee shop. People live close-knit yet isolated lives: they trust each other but resent or fear "outsiders" (which means anyone from over the mountains), and they have their own ways of doing things. Houses are thinly sprinkled among trees and craggy hillsides, property values and tax revenues are lower than in the rest of Marin, and public services are correspondingly sparse. There is a rural self-sufficiency, a kind of heartland independence, among the residents here. It seems odd to find this characteristic perched on the very edge of the Pacific Ocean, as if these people had succeeded in clinging to prairie values in the face of that enormous cauldron of anomie. Perhaps the reason for it can be found in the fact that many West Marin residents are farmers.

When I was growing up in Palo Alto, the tract house I lived in was originally surrounded by fields and orchards. But that setting disappeared when I was about five, eaten up by suburban development. It wasn't until I took on this West Marin assignment, twenty-five years later, that I realized there were still major agricultural pockets in the San Francisco Bay Area. The first few times I drove out of San Francisco and over to Tomales Bay, I couldn't believe how incredibly rural it was. I don't mean the wilderness areas, like the federally owned Point Reyes National Seashore or the acres of undeveloped land on hillsides around the highway; those I had seen before. I mean the dairy ranches and cattle ranches and horticultural farms that were still being run as family-owned operations.

Most of the families who farmed in West Marin were of Italian ancestry. (Synanon's Maggetti Ranch, obviously, had originally belonged to one such family.) People like the Grassis and the Giacominis were third- and fourth-generation Marin residents, ranging from grizzled old guys with beer bellies and few words to handsome, articulate young men who had studied the latest agricultural techniques at U C Davis. A surprising number of them had what seemed to me to be slight Italian accents—not the harsh Brooklyn Italian accent, but a softened, barely detectable California version—as if they had spoken to no one but their own relatives for the past ninety-five years.

With a few exceptions (an old German-Jewish couple who raised flowers, for instance), most of the agricultural people in West Marin were cattle ranchers, and a high proportion of them raised dairy cattle. West Marin was apparently one of the choice dairy-ranch spots in the state, because its naturally moist, fog-filled climate meant that the ranchers didn't need to use much irrigation; the cows could simply graze off the hillsides all year round. It *had* been a choice spot, that is, until the federal government established the Point Reyes National Seashore in the mid-1960s. What had been a tremendous boon to the rest of us Californians was a hardship for the dairy ranchers, as they helplessly watched acres of prime agricultural land being converted into a wilderness area. By the early 1980s some of them were operating ranches on land temporarily leased back from the government. Others were doubling up with fathers or older brothers, hoping that someday a newly available ranch might make it possible for them to run their own places. Hence the enormous interest when the two Synanon ranches suddenly came on the market. Even the *possibility* that the local foundation might resell one or both, deed restrictions and all, brought out so many West Marin ranchers that we had to organize group tours of the properties.

Before the first of these tours, I called up Sally, my contact at Synanon, to check out the date with her. I had never met Sally in person, only talked to her over the phone, but even so it was clear to me that she was the perfect public relations officer for Synanon, a combination of friendliness, efficiency, and almost invisible guardedness.

"Yes, that will be fine," she said in her crisp British voice. (How did *she* ever hear about Synanon? I wondered.) "How many ranchers did you say—about eight or nine? Fine. Just make sure you all arrive in one group. You can park your cars in the lot at Maggetti, just inside the main gate. I'll tell the guards you'll be here at ten o'clock Thursday morning."

The guards, I had heard, were there to keep people in as well as out. There were stories of Synanon members— teenage boys, I think—who had fled the compound, struggled through the brushy wilderness, and emerged tired and bleeding to beg the neighboring farmers to take them in. These boys apparently reported beatings, starvation techniques, and more exotic tortures as part of the Synanon routine. But they had been recaptured (or so the stories went) by Synanon, which insisted that they were unreliable drug addicts lying about the circumstances of their cure. I wasn't even sure the runaways had ever existed. I only knew about them third-hand, from West Marin residents who knew someone who might have lived near the people who found them, or some such convoluted connection.

And balanced against stories like these were the ones about Synanon's helpfulness to the ranching community:

the time they had sent their fire truck to put out a barn fire when the nearest town's truck was out of commission, the day they had taken a hurt child to the hospital. (West Marin is notoriously short on ambulances.) It was as if Synanon represented Organization, with a capital O, and while that sometimes frightened the locals, they could also see its occasional advantages.

I instructed the ranchers to meet me at Marconi (neutral turf, since Synanon had already vacated it) at nine-thirty, so that we could all drive over to Maggetti together. When the ranchers showed up, they were appropriately dressed in ranch clothes—denim overalls, flannel shirts, heavy work boots. I, as is my wont, was inappropriately dressed in open-toed, high-heeled sandals, black jeans (which pick up every mote of dust), and a silk shirt. They tolerated me.

Sally met us at the Maggetti parking lot, which, in addition to our cars and trucks, held several huge farm vehicles, a school bus, and a number of Synanon-owned cars. A woman close to my own age, with an attractive if somewhat severe face, Sally wore denim overalls, heavy boots, and a haircut about a quarter of an inch long. A companion she brought along to help with the tour—a short, round-eyed, middle-aged figure of initially indeterminate sex—wore the same outfit. Both sported silver medallions around their necks. I looked from them to the ranchers and back: except for the medallions, they were dressed identically, even to the haircuts.

One of the ranchers whispered to me, as we trailed behind the rest of the tour, the perhaps apocryphal history of the closely cropped heads. Originally, it seems, head-shaving had been a punishment for drug addicts who broke any of the numerous and strict Synanon rules. Then one day Dederich's son broke a rule and had to have his head shaved. After that Dederich shaved his own head and declared that all Synanon members, male and female, should do the same. It reminded me of a fairy tale, or the old story about how the King of Spain forced his subjects to adopt his lisp.

Sally first took us through the enormous dining room, which was decorated with schlock chandeliers and egregiously ugly wall mosaics. Then she led us to an institutional kitchen larger than anything I have ever seen, before or since: rows and rows of gleaming metal stove-and-oven units and metal counter spaces sat in front of ten-foot-high wall-unit refrigerators. The dairy ranchers professionally admired the refrigeration capacity, and then we moved on to the dwelling spaces. Prefab units furnished with bunk beds and cheap plywood doors, they had ceilings made of some kind of blotchy rough material, as if someone had thrown mud or mortar upward from the ground and let it stick. In the children's rooms, an occasional crayon drawing was taped to the walls; otherwise the decor was exceedingly bare, though an iconographic photo of Dederich and his wife hung just beside one of the exits. As we walked in and out of the various

buildings, Katie—it turned out that was the indeterminate person's name—kept up a constant stream of barely
pertinent conversation with whoever happened to be
near her. It struck me that she had been assigned to "help"
Sally for her own benefit and not Sally's.

"What's that?" One of the ranchers was pointing to a
giant polyhedron with an arched roof that Sally had
walked right past.

"Oh, that's our Stew room," she said. "I'm afraid I can't
take you in there." I recalled the horrific Stew descrip-
tions published by disaffected ex-members, and pictured
Satanic rites taking place at that very moment in the holy
of holies. But as far as I could tell from the outside, the
building was completely unoccupied.

She led us along the tanbark path to the "factory" (deserted now, but formerly filled with pencil-packers, box-
assemblers, and other employees in the office-supply
industry) and then to the barns. "A lot of these structures
would have to go," I heard one rancher mutter to another.
"Taxes would be too high if you kept them all."

We passed an enormous stack of firewood—an army's
ten-year supply, or so it seemed to my uneducated eyes.

"Why so much wood?" I asked.

"Oh, some of our people got interested in survivalist
doctrines, and we decided to have at least a year's supply
of everything on hand," Sally answered. "But the wood's
not worth trucking away, so we're just leaving it here."

"Comes free with the ranch, eh?" one of the men asked, interested only in the practical implications. I, however, had gone off on a train of thought about survivalists. Weren't they the ones, I vaguely wondered, with the caches of guns in their rural hideouts? (Remember, this was fifteen years before Waco and the Michigan Militia; to anyone outside California, my suspicions would have sounded like just another brand of West Marin paranoia.) I tried to banish the thought. But there was undeniably something creepy about the place. Perhaps, I reasoned, it was only that it was so empty. Most of the Synanon membership had already moved to the new compound, at an isolated spot near a small California town called Badger.

When we finished with Maggetti we got in our cars and drove across the highway to Walker Creek. More prefab buildings, more bare bunks, more hot, dry, dusty ground. It reminded me of nothing so much as sleep-away summer camp—even in terms of the way certain places were obviously designated for certain functions, to be performed at prearranged times of day: the bunk house, the rec area, the craft building, the dining room. Again, the issue was Organization. But sleep-away camp was for children, and this was supposed to be a community of adults.

By now everybody was getting hot and tired. The ranchers had seen all they needed to. "Is there any place we can get something to drink?" they asked.

"Of course," said Sally, and conducted us to a dining room much like the one on Maggetti, but smaller and less formal, less "elegant" (if sprayed-on insulation and folding chairs can be said to have degrees of elegance). The choices were water and tea. I chose tea, and sat down at a table where Katie was talking to three of the ranchers.

"So you see, I come from eight generations of character disorder," she chirped, smiling up at the grey-haired rancher next to her, staring into his face with her bright, round eyes. He smiled back and patted her hand, which was resting on the table, then silently picked up his water glass in both his own hands. I excused myself and went to the bathroom, which Sally had pointed out as we came in. The door to the bathroom was labeled "Examiner," and it took me a while to figure out the joke: the San Francisco *Examiner* was the paper that had really gone after Synanon about the rattlesnake. I went into a cubicle, sat down, and reached up to lock the door. There was no lock. That was the Synanon rule, no locks on any doors. Everybody must be available at all times, I thought, for scrutiny by the omnipresent eye of the Examiner.

———

After the tour was over, the ranchers told me that Maggetti would make a great dairy ranch, but Walker Creek was too flat and too dry. In the end the foundation sold Maggetti to a Marin-born rancher of Italian descent and divided Walker Creek up among several deserving nonprofit groups. The Marconi Property sat empty for a number of years, waiting to be developed into something useful—just as it had waited eighty years earlier, filled with visions of a brave new technology, for Marconi himself to arrive. Meanwhile, Dederich lived out his "retirement" in Badger, dying of old age just a few years ago. And West Marin is still largely agricultural.

In the "strange meeting" of Wilfred Owen's war poem, the dreamer finds his ghosts coming to life:

Then, as I probed them, one sprang up, and stared
With piteous recognition in fixed eyes,
Lifting distressful hands, as if to bless . . .
"I am the enemy you killed, my friend."

Nothing quite that dramatic happens when I think back on the encounter between the agriculturalists and the cultists. Still, even without the wartime guilt Owen was evoking, I am aware of an uncanny discomfort associated with this memory. At the time, I know, I vaguely viewed Synanon as "the enemy," and there was certainly more than a little fear mingled with my curiosity. What surprises me now, as I look back and examine those weird Synanon spirits who so hated to be examined, is how ambivalently sympathetic I feel toward them.

In the stereotypical vision of California (in my own

stereotypical vision, I should say), the rural ranchers are the good guys—the real thing—and the kooky ideologues are the unwelcome outsiders. But that encounter forced me to question that simple opposition. In a funny way, Synanon and the ranchers had more in common with each other than I did with either of them. They both existed as relatively self-sustaining communities, isolated from the urban center less than an hour away. They both had gripes against the federal government (the ranchers for the loss of Point Reyes, Synanon because of IRS trouble). And they both premised their form of life on a daily commitment to hard physical labor and a strict attention to the correct way of doing things. Oddly enough, this very rigidity seems to have been what made it possible for them to exercise a generous degree of tolerance, both toward each other and toward the eighth-generation character disorders they made a home for.

I don't mean to be romantic about this. Certainly the ranchers were glad enough to see Synanon go, if only because it freed up prime agricultural land. But if Synanon had stayed, the West Marin ranching community would probably have continued to get along with its odd neighbors just fine. It occurs to me now that the strangeness of their encounter, which struck me so heavily at the time, was almost invisible to them. What I saw as a meeting of California opposites was to them just another real estate tour.

REPORT ON A SITE VISIT

T oward the end of my period with the foundation, at the request of the director of arts programming, I drove out to Bolinas to check on the filmmaker who had asked for half a million dollars.

I was not in favor of this visit. "It will only encourage him," I had said, riffling through the stack of letters and phone messages that had already accumulated in his file. "And what are we doing to do *after* I make the site visit?"

"If you do not feel that the project is compelling," said the arts director, raising an eyebrow—he was a stickler for observing the forms of apparent objectivity—"then we will write to him and say that. But after our failure to get back to him properly, he at least deserves a site visit."

Part of the problem is that I don't like that drive: ten miles of winding road, much of the way with no protective railing between you and a nine-hundred-foot drop to the ocean. For days before making the trip, I dreamed of that sickening fall, of my car swooping over the edge as the brakes failed. I even took the car to a mechanic to get the brakes checked before I went.

As it always turns out, the *real* danger of this drive is the high probability that you will get behind some old duffer who drives at fifteen miles an hour and lurches unpredictably at curves. Mine had one rear brakelight out, which meant I was constantly expecting him to turn right, or at least pull over for me. No such luck. I could almost feel an ulcer growing.

I reached Bolinas early anyway, since I habitually leave extra time to arrive at appointments, get to movies, meet trains, or catch planes. I hate being late, and I hate it when other people are. I've nearly lost friendships over delays of a mere quarter-hour.

When, as prearranged, I called the victim of my visit (let's label him Mr. Coniglio to protect his true identity), only his machine was home. "I'm either deep in my creative work, walking on the beach, or just having *too* good a time to come to the phone," it sneered. "So leave a message and I'll get back to you."

"This is Wendy Lesser from the foundation," I enunciated. (Have you ever noticed how strange your own name sounds when you have to recite it into a machine?) "I'm a bit early. I'll call you again in half an hour."

To while away the time, I strolled through the local bookshop, where I could find only nature guides and metaphysical guidance. "I've finally found a book on meditation that expresses my own attitude exactly," I overheard a customer telling the cashier. "It basically says that whatever you believe in will work for you."

I crossed the street to the local café and ordered coffee with yogurt cheesecake. Jam smears festooned my table and flies buzzed around my head. One dropped into my nearly empty coffee cup. I got up to try the phone again.

"John Paul Coniglio," he answered for himself.

"Hello, Mr. Coniglio—it's Wendy Lesser from the foundation. I'm in a phone booth in downtown Bolinas."

"Oh, the one next to the café? Great. Listen, I'll be right down to get you. And while you're waiting, why don't you go two doors over to the Bolinas Art Association gallery and take a look at my photos? It's my first public show. I'll meet you there."

Unwillingly, but still imbued with a site-visit sense of obligation, I wandered into the gallery. It was deserted. Most of the photos were sunsets in black and white, rainy landscapes, or raggedly dressed, imploringly pathetic children. Mr. Coniglio's pictures stood out: a number of studies of "my girlfriend at the beach" (a goose-pimpled breast and nipple against a twilight sky, the curve of a naked hip against sand), and one frontal photo of a nude man in an armchair entitled "Self-Portrait." The man had rather wild though wispy blond hair and washed-out blue eyes. His penis drooped prominently in the foreground.

I hurried away so as not to be standing just there when

the original walked in, as he soon did. He looked less robust and slightly saner than in the picture. I've noticed
that people often do look saner with their clothes on.

"Well, did you like them?"

"Very interesting," I mumbled. "Shall we go talk about
your proposal now?"

He led me up the hill on foot, having expressed shock
that I might want to drive my car anywhere. ("Leave it
right here—it will be fine," he said, but I already didn't
trust him, and envisioned the car towed to the nearest
large town, myself stranded forever in Bolinas.) On the
way up the hill, he recited the lunch possibilities: some
soup he had made, a little salad, did I want to stop for
some cheese? No, well, then we could just eat the soup,
but . . .

"I'm not really very hungry," I interrupted, "and since
we only have a limited amount of time, I think we should
spend it talking about your work."

"Oh." He seemed very disappointed. "I thought you
were going to be able to stay for the whole afternoon."

"No, I have to get back to the office for a meeting," I
lied, "so I won't be able to stay more than an hour, or at
most an hour and a half."

"Well, this is it." He unlocked the door to a weather-
beaten little bungalow, part of a complex of destitute-
looking buildings perched halfway up the hill. They all
had beautiful ocean views from their rickety porches.

His "studio" consisted of a large-ish room that encompassed a kitchen area and a floor-level bed covered
by the regulation Indian bedspread, with a smaller
room—his "office"—leading off the kitchen. The smell of
the place was close and oppressive, as if several pairs of
sexually active old shoes and socks had been closeted together for weeks. This atmosphere was aggravated by
the additional smell of gas when Mr. Coniglio turned on
the stove to warm the soup.

"While we're waiting for that to heat up, come in and
take a look at my files."

Madmen always have files, or at any rate madmen of a
certain sort, the ones who seek to organize experience by
chronicling and alphabetizing every idea that floats
through their minds, every act of real or supposed injustice committed against them, every seed of potential
enormous wealth. Mr. Coniglio's office was lined with
boxes and boxes of index cards. He began pulling them
out in order, explaining the contents of each one. "And
these are some notes for films I've jotted down in the middle of the night . . . and here are some ideas for grant proposals . . ." I calculated that we were going to be about
halfway finished with the boxes by nightfall.

"Mr. Coniglio, I—"

"Call me John Paul."

"John Paul. I just wanted to say that since my time here
is limited, perhaps it would be better if you summarized

your overall plans. I mean, I will gain a great deal more insight into your work if you tell me directly what you'd like to do, in a general sort of way, rather than giving me all this detailed information. It's all very interesting, of course, but there's only so much I can absorb at once, so you'd do better to get your big ideas across first."

"Oh. Well, what do you want to hear about? The Wilhelm Reich film I mentioned in my letter?"

"Yes, that would be fine. Tell me why you feel it's an important film to make."

"Do you know anything about Wilhelm Reich?"

Suddenly I was the one on the defensive. "Well, I've heard of him, of course," I hedged. "Ozone boxes, wasn't it?"

"*Org*one. You obviously aren't very familiar with his work. He was one of the great geniuses of the century, a persecuted man who was hounded to death because his ideas were too new and too overpowering for people to accept."

"Isn't the—er—do you smell gas leaking somewhere?"

"That's just the soup cooking."

"Oh. I thought the flame might have gone out." I wondered if I had an obligation to bring the conversation back to Reich, then decided I didn't. "What kind of work are you doing now, exactly?"

"You mean my *real* work, or what I do to support myself?"

"For support."

"Well, right now I'm working as a janitor at Lucasfilm. I'm going to work my way up through the ranks. I got the job through Kelly Girls. When I signed up, I told them, 'Give me anything that comes along at Lucasfilm.' And sure enough, this job came along. I believe in fate. Though I almost didn't get the job. At the interview, the guy told me I was overqualified. I was almost in tears by the time I left, and I was depressed all the next day. But then he called me and said if I wanted the job, I could have it. So far I'm just sweeping floors and cleaning bathrooms, but I know things will look up soon."

I was growing increasingly nauseated and began to fear I might faint. Something in that room was certainly interfering with my breathing. Since my anxiety attacks are not usually psychosomatic in nature, I still suspected the gas stove. I could picture myself collapsing on the floor, losing consciousness, absorbing foul gases (my understanding of what comes out of a gas stove is relatively primitive), and gradually rendering up my meager store of oxygen. Days later they would find my car and eventually trace me to Coniglio's studio. "Yes, we saw her walking up the hill with him," the neighbors might volunteer, "but she was carrying a briefcase. It all looked very official. And he's never given us any trouble before."

"Excuse me, I just have to get a breath of fresh air." I barged past him out to the porch and stood leaning against the railway, gulping pure breaths.

"Oh" came from inside. "You were right. The pilot light *has* gone out on the stove. But I've fixed it now." He emerged onto the porch, smiling.

I held my corner, guarding my position like a prize-fighter. He'd fooled me once, but he wasn't going to lure me back inside again so easily.

"I have another film idea about radiation. Robert Red-ford's very interested in it . He had the script for about a year, and then he finally returned it with a nice note say-ing he was going with another script on the same topic, but to keep in touch. A few months after that I had a dream about him, and when I wrote to say I thought it was some kind of sign, I got another letter from him. He said he had had similar experiences, and he hoped we would continue to collaborate spiritually. I still have the letter."

"Can I see it?" An edge of suspicion must have crept into my voice, because he suddenly became defensive.

"Of course. Why not? Come inside and I'll show you a whole folder of stuff."

The other thing about madmen, aside from their files, is that they can always trick you into doing what they want. I was still the foundation's representative, and I hadn't completed my site visit. It would have been too bizarre to refuse; I had to follow him in.

"Okay, but I really have to leave soon," I warned. "Just show me the most important stuff."

From a shelf in the kitchen/bedroom he took down two enormous folders and a cardboard box of the sort that, before the age of computers, high-quality typewriter paper used to come in. He opened one of the folders and peered in.

"Here's some of the material I xeroxed for you. It begins with my earliest work and moves up to my most recent proposals. The first page, as you can see—"

"Great, I'll take it with me," I said, practically ripping the folder out of his hands. It was a difficult choice—either to keep my distance and let him drone on, or move in for the grab—but, even at the expense of caution, I couldn't bear going through every page with him.

"And this," he said, eyeing me somewhat strangely, "is everything connected to my dealings with your foundation." He opened the second folder and leafed through it until he came to a single-spaced typed document that covered several pages. "This, for instance, is one of my letters to your director. Sometimes when I wake up in the middle of the night I get ideas I want to communicate with him, so I just begin typing them out. This is one of about thirty I have on file, and of course there are countless others still bubbling around in my head."

Those of us who have lived through the assassination years of American history know very well what to think of masses of unsent letters addressed to persons in positions of prominence or authority. I made a mental note to warn the director of his potential danger. At the same time, I resolved to have him sign the rejection letter we would have to send this guy, since his name was already on the hit list and I still had a chance to remain somewhat anonymous—a chance, I mused, that was rapidly diminishing with every moment I remained in the presence of the soon-to-be-denied applicant.

"Weren't you going to show me Robert Redford's note?" I asked, and then immediately realized my mistake. In his inability to locate this obviously fictitious missive, he might become painfully frustrated and unleash his frustration in violence. I cursed myself for what one Berkeley friend calls my "unremittingly linear" mind.

Luckily John Paul Coniglio was not subject to the same constraints of linearity. He eased us out of the uncomfortable juncture I had created by ignoring my remark and leaping to an entirely new subject.

"Let me show you something amazing. Do you believe in psychic phenomena?"

Since I felt that both his opinion and my own were too predictable to warrant expression, I merely smiled politely. Besides, the fewer points of difference I raised, the better this conversation would go and the sooner it would be over. I was amazed that this tactic had not occurred to me earlier.

"See this book?" From his highest shelf he took down

an old green volume entitled *Telepathy.* "I found it in a bookstore in Santa Cruz while I was there visiting my brother. I had vaguely been thinking of writing something on telepathy anyway, so I was interested enough to pick up the book. And when I opened it up, look what I found."

He showed me the inside front cover, on which "John Paul Coniglio" was inscribed in handsome cursive writing.

"That's not my signature," he said.

"Are you sure?"

This was not a good response. He evidently resented my distrust.

"Of course I'm sure. *This* is my handwriting." He held out the front sheet of one of his proposals, which had "Jack Coniglio" written in the corner. It was indeed a different signature.

"Why Jack instead of John Paul?" I asked, finding myself unable to resist the illogical logic of the conversation.

"Well, that's an interesting story. I used to call myself Jack all the time. In fact, Paul isn't even my official middle name. John Paul Coniglio was my grandfather's name, and a few years ago I began to hear his voice telling me to adopt his name. He died when I was twelve," he added parenthetically. "Anyway, I ignored it for a long time. Then one day I went to pick up my shoes at the neighborhood shoe repair—this was when I still lived in San Francisco—and the old Italian lady behind the counter took my ticket and said, 'Ah, Mr. Coneelio'—she pronounced it the way my grandfather had, without the G. 'No, it's Conig-lio,' I said (that's how I pronounced it at the time), and she said, 'Yes, Mr. Coneelio.' And right then I knew it must be a sign. It was my grandfather again, speaking to me through this old lady. So I gave in."

"Well, Mr. Coniglio—I mean, John Paul," I said, looking at my watch and edging toward the door. "It's about time for me to go now. If I don't leave within the next five minutes, I'll be late for my meeting." The life-after-death routine had been the last straw. People who have beliefs like that—fundamentalists, born-agains, reincarnationists, and so forth—tend to be a lot more cavalier, I've noticed, about the loss of anyone's *first* life.

"But we've hardly had a chance to talk at all! What's the point of coming all the way out here if you're not going to listen to my plans? I bet you're not even going to give me the grant!"

"Honestly, it's not my decision. That will be decided entirely by other people. I won't be in on it in any way, except to report that I've seen you and that you certainly seem to have all the preparation you need to carry out the project. But, John Paul," I interrupted myself in the headlong effort at self-preservation, pausing in front of the door, "I do think I should warn you that the chances aren't great. The foundation doesn't give grants to *any* individuals at present, and it almost never supports films, so there would have to be very unusual circumstances to make them come up with the money for your project. And, frankly, I just don't think they're going to do it. That's not an informed judgment, but it's my considered opinion, based on what I know about how they work." I was busily wedging as many pronouns as I could between myself and the operations of this devious organization.

He watched me silently for a few moments as I backed out the door. I gave a feeble wave, then turned and strode rapidly down the path.

"You mean they sent you all the way out here to talk to me for nothing?" he suddenly shouted. "You know, I think they never had any intention of giving me a grant. But still they made me spend all this time talking to you, and got my hopes up and everything. That's a shitty thing to do!" He sounded ready to cry.

I felt suitably guilty. I *was* guilty. Even in my hell-bent effort at survival, even as I fled Bolinas never to return, I was compelled to admit, if only to myself, that this madman's complaint was the sanest comment that had been made all day, by either of us.

And now, looking back on the experience, I realize that there was another level to the discomfort as well. Even then I must have sensed, if only subconsciously, that this struggling pseudo-artist with his day job as a janitor bore a crude, parodic, but nonetheless structurally sound resemblance to me, the foundation-employed editor of a literary publication so small and impecunious as to be practically imaginary. We both harbored grandiose ambitions; we both saw gainful employment as a necessary but distasteful distraction from our real pursuits. If I feel, from the vantage point of a subsequent decade, that my aspirations have now been proven rational whereas his still sound downright crazy, that is not enough to blind me to the fact that we once appeared to be siblings in folly. However much I might like to attribute the divergence in our fates entirely to skill and sense, I am forced to acknowledge the crucial role played by chance. Nor does this realization make me any kinder or more generous to people like John Paul Coniglio when I meet them today. On the contrary, it cements me in my stony resistance, for they represent in my mind the horrible drop to the ocean, the potential fall that lies just to the side of the road I happen to be on.

FOUNDING A MAGAZINE

U ntil I was twenty-seven, I had no idea I was intended to be an editor. Editing is not the sort of thing they discuss in high school vocational seminars or teach in college courses, and even if they did no one would be interested in pursuing it. It has a kind of indefinability, a behind-the-scenes lack of tangible glamour. One doesn't naturally absorb dramatic tales about becoming an editor, even when one has read them. Only long after the fact—long after I had become an editor myself—did I realize that one of the formative books of my youth, Leonard Woolf's autobiography, had been in part about founding a literary press.

My own editing career began without Hogarthian ambitions. I just wanted to take the next step up on the little literary ladder I happened to be occupying at that moment. For a year or two I had been writing monthly book reviews for a local organ called the *San Francisco*

Review of Books, which ranged in quality from the somewhat interesting to the truly atrocious (ranged within
each issue, I mean). Like an actor eyeing the director's
role, I was curious to see what editing was like, so I asked
the founding editor of the *SFRB*—a strangely bland,
surprisingly unliterary, lackadaisical but nonetheless
persistent guy—whether he would let me guest-edit
an issue. If some twenty-seven-year-old know-nothing
came to *me* with such a request, I would sputter an in-
dignant no, but this editor was nonchalantly agreeable.
He gave me the August 1979 issue, which otherwise
wouldn't have appeared (he always took his vacation in
August), and told me to do whatever I wanted.

The first thing I did was to contact a bunch of writers.
Some of them were already amply published: Christopher Ricks, who had propelled me in this professional direction; Thom Gunn, whose recent book of poetry I had
reviewed for a UC Berkeley newspaper; and my mother,
Millicent Dillon, whose two books of fiction were soon
to be followed by a highly regarded biography of Jane
Bowles. I also borrowed one writer from the *SFRB*'s
stable—the theater critic Irene Oppenheim, whose
firmly opinionated columns I had admired. For the rest
I resorted to college and graduate-school friends. To
read now through that Table of Contents is, for me, to re-
visit the scenes of my youth. Among the listed writers
are two college boyfriends, one of my Harvard tutors,

four graduate-school comrades (not to mention my business partner, Katharine), a freelance journalist who was one of my first Berkeley friends, and even a one-time employer of mine from the Oakland Office of Community Development. I slaved away on that single issue, spending months getting it all in shape. I had never before chosen headline fonts, or proofread columns of type, or done page layout, but I learned on the job. Halfway through the process I discovered that the *SFRB* editor had no money in the magazine's budget to print the issue I was working on. Undeterred, I sold ads, raided my savings account, and found a printer who was willing to give me a bargain rate on a tiny print-run. For the last few days before publication I worked in the magazine's North Beach offices from early morning to late at night, laboriously pasting up each tabloid-sized page on its piece of thin, white, blue-lined cardboard. Exhausted and near tears, I only took a break to eat lunch in a nearby Chinese restaurant, where one of my fortune-cookies carried the disheartening message "For better luck, wait until spring." (A few months later I told this story to Vikram Seth, who immortalized it in his verse-novel *The Golden Gate*. But I am getting ahead of myself.)

I was exhausted, but I was also deeply engaged, and by the time the magazine came off the presses I was determined to edit my own literary review. I stole Irene

Oppenheim away from the *SFRB*, alerted all the other writers that I would be expecting repeat performances, and set the beginning of 1980 as the first publication date. I made a list of about ten possible names for the new magazine on an index card, and from among them I chose *The Threepenny Review* for its obvious Brechtian overtones, and also because I thought it sounded nice. (A few years ago I again came across that index card: among the other names on it were *Washington Square*—for reasons which will be apparent to you—and *Wigan Pier*, in honor of George Orwell.) I decided that the magazine would appear in tabloid format because that was the only form I knew how to paste up, and I got it designed, at a seriously discounted rate, by a typesetter I had met on my first consulting job in Berkeley. In those early months I depended heavily on Irene, a veteran of many start-up organizations; together we sent out hundreds of subscription forms and drove around the Bay Area visiting dozens of bookstores. To a certain extent these methods succeeded, and in January of 1980 the magazine was launched.

In literary terms, *The Threepenny Review* grew easily and steadily. By the second issue I had met Vikram Seth—then an economics student at Stanford—and had published his first poem. Gore Vidal, in response to my importuning letter, appeared in the sixth issue. (With his typical dry wit, he had agreed to write for this nearly invisible publication because he was running for senator from California and needed the visibility.) John Berger, Paul Bowles, and Robert Coles all showed up in the eighth issue; by this time I was paying the princely sum of twenty-five dollars per article. Meanwhile Thom Gunn had become a regular contributor, as had Leonard Michaels, with whom I had taken two courses at Berkeley. The two of them brought in a number of other writers, including, over the years, Robert Hass, August Kleinzahler, W. S. Di Piero, Robert Pinsky, Diane Johnson, and Susan Sontag—each of whom, in turn, drew in friends and colleagues, so that the circle was continuously widening. And mountains of unsolicited manuscripts poured in, from which I unearthed the likes of Lars Eighner, Sigrid Nunez, and Dagoberto Gilb, not to mention already established writers like Phillip Lopate, Mary Gordon, and Vivian Gornick.

Financially, things were not so simple. At the beginning, every month's bills caused me enormous angst: I couldn't see how I was going to go on paying them, yet I couldn't bear the idea of terminating the infant magazine. But by the end of the first year *Threepenny* was beginning to get some small grants, and subscriptions had grown to over a thousand. After ten years I got a larger grant which allowed me to pay myself a nominal salary for the first time, and twelve years into the magazine's history I finally got enough to hire a half-time assistant—a young writer named Lisa Michaels who steered us through the shoals of software and hardware acquisition into the smoother waters of desktop publishing, and who became, in the course of five years, a treasured colleague rather than a hired hand. *The Threepenny Review*, which now has about nine thousand readers, is still run by a paid staff of only one and a half people; and it still operates out of the apartment I lived in when I started it.

The satisfactions of this work are, of course, balanced by its demands. There is inevitably a great deal of busywork involved in putting out a magazine—work like data entry, proposal writing, postage metering, package wrapping, trips to the printer, trips to the mailing house, trips to the recycling center—and when the staff is as small as ours is, nobody gets out of the boring jobs. But since it is busywork done for my own purposes, I don't mind it much. Whenever I have to label and seal a huge pile of renewal notices, I think to myself: Well, it's better than having to attend a department meeting. In my cheerier moods I can even feel somewhat grateful for the abundance of relatively mindless tasks, which keep me occupied during the hours and days when I'm not up to thinking hard.

Everyone who has ever worked as a literary editor loves the discovery element of the job—those moments when you open an envelope, read the first words of a new writer, and know you have hit paydirt. I too enjoy this, but there are other aspects of editing a magazine that give me, if anything, even more pleasure. I love, for instance, the process of ordering the pieces in a given issue, deciding which ones will come first and last, creating the train of subterranean connection that leads through the issue from one essay to another, from a story to its accompanying poem. And I love the satisfyingly tactile job of pasting up the ads and pictures in their final places, once the desktop-published pages have been run out of the computer. But most of all, I think, I love the actual process of editing: taking a piece of writing that is *almost* there and making it come clear, like a photographic image submerged in developer. It requires a kind of negative capability that I wouldn't have thought someone of my character would have. You read the story or the essay (I can't really do it with poetry) and lend yourself to the effort that the piece itself is making; you discern, within the body of the manuscript, the lineaments of its own perfect form. And then you tell the author, and both of you are pleased.

I suppose I could have been happy with other forms of literary self-employment. (Early in my *Threepenny* career I cut out a cartoon from *The New Yorker* that showed a king sitting on a throne and talking to a scribe. "Most of all," he is saying, "I enjoy being able to work at home.") But there is something particularly satisfying about the mixture involved in editing and publishing a literary re-view—a combination of businesslike planning and artis-tic responsiveness, long-term consideration and snap decision-making, efficiency and laziness, gossip and pri-vacy, reading and looking . . . It is, in short, a combina-tion of many of the things I like and all the things I am.

DRAFTED

B eing part of the underpaid, overworked army of literary aspirants and arbiters entails certain civic responsibilities. And one of those responsibilities, if you have acquired sufficient visibility in your field and insufficient chutzpah to decline the invitation, is service on an NEA "peer review" panel. For many years I had mixed feelings about the individual literary fellowships given by the National Endowment for the Arts. In this, I was not alone. Nearly all writers in America had mixed feelings about these fellowships, because nearly all writers found that every year, when they read the lists of those given awards, many crucial names were missing—their own names, the names of their closest literary friends, and the names of more famous American writers whose work they admired. Instead, mingled in with a few recognizable names, were veritable legions of total strangers who had each been awarded $20,000 by the NEA. What gave? How did the NEA come up with these cockamamie lists?

These were the negative feelings in the mix. On the positive side was a general sense that it was good for the American government to show its support for the country's writers, symbolically as well as actually (even if this support came in the form of a literature budget smaller than that of a medium-sized European city like Munich—even if the *whole* NEA budget was less than what the Defense Department paid for its 102 military bands). Also, we were all forced to admit that *some* talented people squeezed through the selection process, getting a $20,000 leg up just at the point when they could really use the help. And then there was the fact that conservative congressmen hated the NEA with a passion. Anything that bugged Jesse Helms couldn't be *all* bad.

Thus far, my ambivalent feelings about government-sponsored literary grants were probably typical of people in my professional and educational circles. But complicating the mix were other sentiments from further back, having to do with the household I grew up in. From the time I was about ten or eleven, my mother had been a struggling fiction-writer. Before that she had pursued a number of other careers, including physicist, dance therapist, Democratic Party organizer, and free-lance journalist. But around the same period when she met my stepfather (a relatively brief presence in our lives who came and went when I was in early adolescence, leaving behind as his only tangible legacy my mother's new, euphonious, and highly literary-sounding name), she decided to begin taking herself seriously as a writer. By the year I started college she had earned a master's degree in creative writing, published a book of short stories with Viking, been invited to several writers' colonies, and begun to be recognized as one of Northern California's resident literary figures.

At the same time, what I remember about my childhood is that we were always short of money. We were by no means poor: we lived, after all, in the upper-middle-class splendor of Greenmeadow, where we had access to a membership-only community pool and an array of neighborhood services. My sister and I were always given music lessons, dance lessons, art lessons; our house was filled with books, and we were even taken occasionally to the theater (a luxury that now seems prohibitively expensive to most professional-class families). For any kind of art, that is, money could usually be found. But for the more routine pleasures of suburban existence— eating out in restaurants, going on vacations, buying a new car—there was never quite enough. This probably had more to do with the fact that my mother was a single parent, back in the days before divorce was common in California, than with the fact that she was a writer; even my father's generous child-support allocation was not enough to bring us up to the income level of our white-collar, intact-family neighbors. But in my mind the two struggles—my mother's struggle to make a career in literature and her financial struggle to make a life in our expensive surroundings—became joined together. It was therefore impressed on me, powerfully if subliminally, that writers needed and deserved a handout.

———

With something like this complex of feelings bubbling around in me, I agreed in the spring of 1993 to serve on the selection panel for that year's round of NEA poetry fellowships. Clinton had recently been elected to the White House. Bush's puppet arts director had resigned, and the search was on for a strong-minded, highly visible NEA director (which they soon got, in the form of Jane Alexander). Recent NEA panelists had made it clear that it was unacceptable for panel selections to be overturned for political reasons. The signs all seemed to point to a new and improved NEA, which perhaps explains why I so readily accepted the invitation to serve on the panel—that, and the $6,000 they offered me to do the job.

It turned out to be a well-paid but hard-earned salary. Over the summer of 1993, when most of my work took place, I put in the equivalent of a month's work (that is, twenty-two or twenty-three full, eight-hour days) reading and commenting on poetry manuscripts. Overall, the NEA had received nearly 2,500 applications for fellowships that year; they came from all fifty states, plus the District of Columbia, the Virgin Islands, Puerto Rico, and Americans living abroad. The poetry submissions amounted to about half that total—1,247, to be exact— and my share of these initially included more than four hundred manuscripts, each consisting of up to ten pages of poetry identified only by application number (no name recognition allowed). I had to select from these enormous boxfuls of material the sixteen manuscripts I liked best, which would be forwarded to an October meeting for full-group discussion with my eight fellow panelists. I also, in the next phase of the operation, read and commented on about fifty more manuscripts which had already passed through someone else's Phase One approval, but this was a much less onerous task, mainly because I did not at that point have the weighty responsibility of eliminating people from the final round of discussion.

I am not and have never been a poet. My qualifications for serving on this panel stemmed from my thirteen years of editing *The Threepenny Review*, which published, and still publishes, a healthy selection of poems in each issue. "Healthy" in my view means more than the sickly few—two or three at most—offered by a general-interest magazine like *The New Yorker*, but fewer than the dangerous overdose you are likely to get in a purely literary magazine like *American Poetry Review, Pequod*, or the *Spoon River Quarterly*. To arrive at my healthy ten or twelve a quarter, I read at least five thousand poems a year. I like and sometimes even love good poetry, as an amateur; but I hate bad poetry with the zeal that only a professional reader can command.

On average, my batch of NEA applicant poems were at a noticeably higher literary level than the unsolicited manuscripts I read each week for *Threepenny*. This should come as no surprise: to apply for an NEA fellowship, a poet needs to have published in at least five different magazines over the previous several years, whereas to send work to *Threepenny* you need only have a postage stamp. (Actually, two postage stamps: one to send the manuscript, and one to get it back.) But even with the quality assurance, there were still quite a few dazzling blunders in the NEA group. And even among the patently *good* poems, it became hard, after about the hundred-and-fiftieth manuscript, to evaluate the work's originality or conscious allusiveness or metrical skill or metaphorical inventiveness. I was beginning to feel that I just didn't have enough in me to cope with appreciating all these different styles; unlike Walt Whitman, I do not contain multitudes. Besides which, they were all beginning to blur together in my mind. "If John Keats were in this pile, I would miss him," I announced to my husband one evening. "The NEA could save a lot of money by just throwing all the manuscripts down the stairs and rewarding the ones that get to the bottom."

That was the low point. Once I got to Washington in October, for the three-day meeting with my fellow panelists, I realized that I had actually been accomplishing something during those solitary weeks and months. The batch of 144 manuscripts that we were to discuss together was markedly better than my own unsorted group had been; some of my favorite poems were things that had not even been in my initial batch, but had been rescued by someone else. And I was relieved, when I met my fellow panelists, to see that I needn't have worried so much about my biases and innate preferences, for their approaches to poetry were various enough to counter my own narrowness of taste. In fact, we had all been *selected* for our differing biases and innate preferences.

I had been expecting the panel to represent racial, gender, geographical, and other forms of distribution, as indeed it did, including two African-American women poets—one young and well educated, one middle-aged and street smart—one Latino poet who also worked as a legal-aid lawyer, a gay male poet and translator, a lesbian poet (I'm counting only those who made their preferences explicit), a southern white male poet with impeccable traditional credentials, a northeastern white male poet with impeccable experimental credentials, a midwestern bookstore owner who happened to be quite familiar with poetry, and me—a white, middle-aged, female Californian. But, as writing this list of adjectives makes clear to me, these categories hardly encompassed our real identities. We had all been chosen for our tastes and our personalities, which were both lively and various. Thanks largely to the intelligent management of our NEA Literature Program "handlers" (I use the word in the most complimentary sense possible), the mix worked.

The NEA people did none of the choosing of manuscripts—in this sense, the process was absolutely free of government influence, or of any administrative cronyism. But they did shape the process: not to favor a particular manuscript or writer but to control the discussion as a whole. I was dreading the three-day panel meeting (I find it a good policy to dread *all* meetings, and then I can very occasionally be pleasurably surprised), but this meeting, though arduous, was consistently fascinating and rewarding. The Literature Program staff had set it up in such a way that we panelists were on for two sessions, off for one, so in between haranguing each other about the virtues of free verse over meter, bare sentiment over technical wizardry, we got to take restorative walks on the grassy Mall, which almost directly adjoins the NEA's building in Washington.

The tone of our discussions only occasionally reached what would technically qualify as a harangue. Mostly we just said our piece and quietly voted. The NEA handlers had supplied each of us with copies of our own written comments on the selected manuscripts, so if you had totally forgotten what you thought during the summer, your own words were there to remind you. This being poetry, our words tended to focus closely on other words, and many of those little comment cards would have been worth publishing as criticism. It was amusing to go around the table and see how the opinions lined up; the alliances were never predictable. The two most experimental poets, for instance, had been selected by the NEA staff to back each other up, but they were the two most often in near-shouting disagreement. I found myself most frequently agreeing with the young black woman poet, and she with me. Nobody consistently backed his or her own ethnic or gender category, to the extent that these things were evident in the poetry—but then, even when it seemed obvious, we were only guessing at the writer's identity.

In fact, the most amusing incident in the whole three days of judging had to do with this kind of guessing at identity. One of the other judges had discovered in her first-round reading a series of linked poems written from the point of view of a young Asian refugee. The style of the poems was simple, pure, and direct. Each of the unrhymed lines began with a capital letter, as they tend to do in the work of novice poets. The imagery was rich—not only with the feel of the home culture's visual wealth but with street scenes from the American city to which the immigrant girl narrator had been transplanted. The

story she told, of lost family members and painful mis-
treatment, was heartrending but somehow never sentimental. The whole manuscript had the feel of real
experience transmuted into true art, and I loved it the
minute I read it. As we went around and discussed it, it
was clear that many other people liked it as well, though
for varying reasons. Some felt the poetry was good but a
little too stilted; some wondered if the sentiment became
sentimentality in the hands of such an obviously young
and inexperienced poet; some felt we should give the
award to her just because she had suffered so much; and
so on. Then the discussion came around the table to the
middle-aged black woman poet.

Let me backtrack and say that on the starting day of
the panel, when this woman first entered the room—
forty-five minutes late, nearly six feet tall, and wearing a
hat and cape of indescribable complexity—I shivered
with anxiety. Oh, no, I thought, she's going to derail the
whole process with some kind of endless political
rhetoric. (Coming from Berkeley makes you prone to
anxiety attacks like these.) As it turned out, she was one
of the best, fairest, and most intelligent panelists I have
ever served with; but she *was* scary. She had, she confided
to me on one of our lunch breaks, been thrown out of her
high school for telling a bunch of the other girls that she
was really an alien from another planet—and making
them *believe* it. This story made sense to me after I saw

her in action on the panel. She could make anybody believe just about anything. (At the end of our three days' work when we asked each other, just as a game, how many of our favorites had gotten fellowships, most of us had about two out of three; *she* had sixteen out of nineteen winners.) Moreover, she had a perfect ear for the music of poetry and could read aloud her selections with insurmountable effectiveness. "No fair!" I interrupted her during one of these renditions. "You could read the *phone book* and make it sound like it deserved a prize!"

Anyway, it was her turn now to comment on the Asian refugee sequence, to put in her two cents about whether this pathetic but talented young girl deserved a prize or didn't. "Well," she said, "I don't think this was written by any young Asian girl. I think it's probably some white male screenwriter giving us his girlfriend's story, or some such thing." Those of us who were in favor of the poem gasped at this, in disbelief or despair. "I've read it over and over again, trying to figure out who wrote it, but I can't," she continued. "And finally I decided: Hey! If he can fool me, more power to him. No matter who wrote it, it's a great poem, and I'm for it. " We all laughed at her then; the response seemed so typical, if atypically wrongheaded.

When we had done all our work, we got to learn the identities of the poets we had selected. ("You would be amazed, maybe even horrified, if you knew how many famous names you've already eliminated," one of the staff members told us encouragingly along the way, when we were stumped about whether we were favoring highly polished poems over the work of inspired newcomers.) Among those we had chosen, it turned out, were the son of a friend of mine, a critic against whom I held a grudge, and a nationally prominent feminist poet—none of whom I had recognized in the blind selection process. The general shortage of well-known names on the NEA lists was partly, we learned, due to elimination: if you'd already won three NEA fellowships in your lifetime, you could no longer apply, so many of the best older poets were ineligible. One of the more famous names to reach our final list was that of a white male poet, author of several published books—and of the heartrending refugee-girl series. When we heard his name announced in conjunction with our cherished poem, we all shrieked in surprise and, a little, in chagrin. Only the Sister from Another Planet could sit calmly and quietly, Cheshire-cat smile adorning her face. She had been right, or as close to right as makes no difference; and she was the only one in the room who had given him the prize for purely literary reasons.

I can't say I was completely happy with the final list of thirty-eight names we came up with. No one on the panel was. We had all lost a few of our favorites, given in to the group judgment when we felt that we alone had been right. Still, I was significantly less *un*happy than I had expected to be. Given the desperation of our task—to cull thirty-eight winners out of 1,247 manuscripts, rewarding only about three percent of the applicants for NEA fellowships—we had done the undoable in a respectable way. We were, in a way, like the ordinary person who walks down the streets of a city giving quarters to the first ten homeless people he meets, and who then has nothing left to give after the first block. It was not our fault that there was not more money to give away, or rather, it was only our fault insofar as we were voting citizens of a country which had decided to spend more on its military bands than its overall arts budget.

On the last day of the panel, while the NEA computer was tallying up our final vote, a large group of us—all but two of the judges, I think—took a long walk over to the Vietnam Memorial. It was a beautifully clear, sunny day, the grass glistened with recent sprinkling, and the trees rustled slightly in the breeze that cooled us on our stroll. When we reached the remarkable black wall, which begins quietly at ground level and then surges up as you walk by its side, I was as moved as I always am by this great piece of public art. And I remember thinking that I could now add to my list of Successful Government Processes (a list that had previously contained only one thing, the selection of Maya Lin's design for the Vietnam Memorial) another item: the NEA poetry panel I had just served on. Given the doubts I had about every element in the process—bureaucratic procedure, committee work, true disinterestedness in the evaluation of poetry, the just deserts of hungry artists, even the nature of philanthropy itself—I felt we had come through with flying colors.

ON PHILANTHROPY

O ne December, seven years into the Reagan era, I started asking people whether or not they gave money to beggars. This was a question which had not troubled me, at least on a conscious level, for many years. Like most residents of Berkeley (perhaps like most residents of any modern American city), I had long since developed a slight frown and a quick shake of the head to shrug off all requests for spare change.

What startled me out of this condition, that December, was a brief encounter in a parking lot not far from home. My little boy and I were crossing from the video rental place to the office supplies store when we were stopped by a heavyset, middle-aged woman. "Excuse me, ma'am, can you spare a quarter?" she said. I did my routine headshake and hustled on.

"What did that lady want?" asked my son, who was then two and a half years old.

"She wanted money," I said.

"*Why* did she want money?" he persisted.

"Because she's poor."

"What's poor?"

With that, my assumptions were brutally jarred out of their comfortable, long-inhabited positions. What I had just done, I realized, was to teach a small child to be hard-hearted. I was creating a monster of unthinking selfishness—or, alternatively, I was presenting myself as a monster of selfishness in the eyes of an innocent, innately tenderhearted child.

Suitably shamed by this encounter, I began to ask my friends and relations about their responses to begging. One California friend, who is in general prone to charitable acts, said he usually tried to give something, though he exercised some discrimination: "For instance, I don't give to the smoking poor." My New York friends, perhaps spurred to a consistency of action by the more profound evidence of need in their city, all seemed to give in one way or another. "If I have any change in my pocket, I give it," said one. "If the request is fairly original, and if it's not aggressive, I generally respond," said another. "I carry five quarters in my pocket whenever I go out, and I give to the first five people who ask that day," said a third. "I carry five one-dollar bills whenever I leave the house, and they're usually gone by the time I get to the corner," said a fourth. (I informed her she was paying over the market rate.)

Finally I asked my husband, "Do you give money to beggars?"

"What is this, a Christmas question?" he growled.

"No, I'm really trying to find out what people do."

"No, I don't give money," he said.

"Why?" I asked.

"Because I was a panhandler once too," he began, "and I know—"

"No," I said. "I mean, what's the philosophical rationale for not giving? I don't give either. But *why* don't we give? What's our justification?"

My husband paused. "Because the government should be doing that, not private citizens," he said.

"Yes," I sighed, relieved at rediscovering the familiar reason.

But my satisfaction didn't last long. A couple of weeks later, this time just before Christmas Day, I was again walking with my little boy on a shopping street near our house when a raggedy, bearded man in a soiled watch cap asked me for money. I snatched at the second chance. "Yes," I said, "just a minute," and I reached into my purse and pulled out two quarters. "Here," I said.

"Thank you, ma'am," he responded—verily, as it seemed to me, tugging on a forelock. "Merry Christmas to you, ma'am. And Merry Christmas to your little boy, too," as he bent down, benignly but still rather frighteningly, over my son.

I felt awful. If anything, I felt worse than when I hadn't given. And that, I realized then, was the impossible situation we had now arrived at. When things get bad enough for some people but not others, when there are poor people in the streets asking you for money, you can't win either way. You can be a malevolent Scrooge or a disgustingly self-congratulatory Lady Bountiful, but you can't remain innocent. No course of behavior is the correct one.

Dickens himself, I think, understood a great deal of this. That's why his philanthropist figures make us so uncomfortable. The Royal Shakespeare Company's 1981 stage production of *Nicholas Nickleby*, for example, tried to stress the enduring social problem over the temporary individual solution by filling the stage with shivering waifs as Nicholas and his family went off to their singularly particular happy ending. A 1987 episode of the television show *The Equalizer* did the same thing: after Robert McCall had saved one homeless family from life in a Times Square flophouse (his self-defined job being merely to protect individual victims), the camera focused its closing shot on a wistful little face, the face of one of the many children still living at the drug-ridden hotel. This type of thing is well-intentioned, but it assuages even as it means to question. Leaving the theater after *Nicholas Nickleby*, or turning to the (hardly less disturbing) eleven o'clock news after *The Equalizer*, we congratulate ourselves on having achieved the proper perspective on the problem. One philanthropist isn't enough; more needs to be done. We can have our sentimentality and eat it too.

In its original form, Dickens's philanthropy is not so easily digestible; it festers and continues to disturb. Because what Dickens is questioning is not just the amount of good any one philanthropist can do, but the very act of philanthropy itself: the gesture of reaching out to save another by means of one's own relative wealth. Inevitably, that gesture is somewhat creepy. This may not always be easy to see in the early and middle novels. With *Bleak House*, for instance, critics often like to contrast the "bad" Mrs. Jellyby (who collects for African relief while neglecting her own family) with the "good" Mr. Jarndyce (who adopts Ada, Richard, and Esther). But in taking this line such critics must be squelching their own instinctive reaction. Isn't there something in the least bit squeamish-making about the way Jarndyce coyly approaches his philanthropic role, and something even more obviously nauseating about the way Esther Summerson devotedly renders him eternal gratitude? You may not be prepared to attribute this effect to Dickens; you may want to view it as an unintentional by-product of his salvational plots, a modern perspective superimposed on a Victorian device. But there is *Great Expectations* to contend with, if you try to hold that view.

In that late, great novel, Dickens laid bare the corruption engendered by the most benign kind of philanthropy. The inexplicable trust fund that brings Pip to London and educates him as a "gentleman" not only cuts him off from beloved friends of his own class (Joe and Biddy) but also distorts his relationships with Miss Havisham (whom he mistakenly believes to be his benefactor, and whom he cravenly submits to as a result) and with the benefactor himself. When Pip discovers that the source of his wealth, education, and new class status is a transported convict, he is filled with disappointment and resentment; he almost hates the man who made him rich. This is not class snobbery alone. It's a result of the discrepancy between what he feels a philanthropist *should* be (a higher type of person, reaching down to help the low) and what his philanthropist *is* (an even lower man who helped Pip climb to success on his back).

In questioning philanthropy as it has affected him, Pip unintentionally casts doubt on the whole enterprise in its more usual (opposite) form. There is something inherently dishonest and unbalanced about the granting and acceptance of "free" money, because the no-strings-attached grant always turns out to be tied quite tightly to the giver. One incurs a debt—of gratitude, of respect, of affection-on-demand—by accepting the gift. In Pip's case it is possible to contrast the relatively honest exchange at the beginning of the novel, when the convict uses fear to extort food and equipment from Pip, with the much more corrupted exchange that takes place when the convict subsidizes Pip's whole life. (What the convict gets, in this exchange, is the satisfaction of having created a gentleman.) In the first case the obligations end with the exchange: Pip carries away his fear, the convict his "wittles" and file. In the second case the obligations are so large and so irrevocable that they can never be paid off, by either party to the arrangement. The convict has made Pip's fortune and ruined, in a sense, his life, while Pip, who at first despises his benefactor for not being someone else, can never fully make up for that initial failure of gratitude.

The real problem with philanthropy is that it calls into question the character of both the donor and the recipient. "Philanthropy is almost the only virtue which is sufficiently appreciated by mankind," Thoreau noted in the first chapter of *Walden*. "Nay, it is greatly overrated; and it is our selfishness which overrates it. A robust poor man, one sunny day here in Concord, praised a fellow-townsman to me, because, as he said, he was kind to the poor; meaning himself." But if selfish egoism is the flaw exposed in the recipient, something not too different also surfaces in the philanthropist, as Thoreau points out in the next paragraph: "Under what latitude reside the heathen to whom we would send light? Who is that intemperate and brutal man whom we would redeem? If anything ail a man, so that he does not perform his functions, if he have a pain in his bowels even,—for that is the

seat of sympathy,—he forthwith sets about reforming—
the world." And to this amusing theory Thoreau appends
a wry and typically ironic self-assessment: "I have never
dreamed of any enormity greater than I have committed.
I never knew, and never shall know, a worse man than
myself." Thoreau's confession has the obviously inten-
tional ring of a boast. In his very moment of rejecting
philanthropy most deeply, of advocating a tend-your-
own-garden technique, he manages (with his habitual
Janus-faced approach to meaning) to echo the kind of
public avowal of one's own sins that typifies one form of
present-day "philanthropist": that is, the TV evangelist.

———

First published in 1854, *Walden* was written at a time
when *philanthropy* still meant something very close to its
Greek roots. The first examples given in the OED, from
the early seventeenth century, show the word being used
strictly in the sense of "love of one's fellow man" (or, by
extension, love of God to man) and the beneficent acts
attached thereunto. This meaning persisted to the middle of the nineteenth century (an 1849 quote, from
Wilberforce, refers piously to "the lessons of universal
Philanthropy"). But by the late nineteenth century the
word had taken on a less spiritual and more pecuniary
meaning. "A great philanthropist has astonished the
world by giving it large sums of money during his lifetime," runs an 1875 entry in the OED; *Harper's Maga-*

zine in 1884 referred to "the head of a great hospital and many philanthropies." This is the sense the word has for us today: it has moved away from a personal and occasionally religious form of giving to a more purely financial one. If one wanted to speak about giving money during the seventeenth, eighteenth, or early nineteenth century, one used instead the word *alms*—or, occasionally, *charity*. *Alms* derives from *eleemosynary*, a word which got its most famous outing (I would venture to say that many people know it only from this context) in the first sentence of Fielding's *Tom Jones*: "An author ought to consider himself, not as a gentleman who gives a private or eleemosynary treat, but rather as one who keeps a public ordinary, at which all persons are welcome for their money." The novelist's mistrust of philanthropy had thus begun by 1749, a good century before Dickens. And the ambivalent feelings attached to charitable giving did not appear only in fiction. Samuel Johnson, in his 1773 Dictionary, defined *alms* straightforwardly enough as "What is given gratuitously in relief of the poor." But he went on to illustrate the word by offering the sentence, "The poor beggar hath a just demand of alms from the rich man; who is guilty of fraud, injustice, and oppression, if he does not afford relief according to his abilities"— which kind of takes the gratuitousness out of "gratuitously." Dr. Johnson also remarked, with his typically digressive sense of the truly interesting, that the word *alms* "has no singular." One cannot give an alm, only alms—again the subliminal sense of obligation and extension (one quarter is not enough . . .).

In fact, all the words associated with philanthropic giving seem afflicted with comparable grammatical eccentricities. *Philanthropy* itself has no verb form (to philanthropize? to philanthrape?), despite the fact that it currently denotes an action. Perhaps that omission came about partly through its origins as a purely spiritual or attitudinal virtue: Johnson defines it as "love of mankind; good nature," both of which can be possessed without necessarily being demonstrated. *Benefactor* (to which Johnson gives the secondary definition "he that contributes to some public charity") also has no verb form, only another noun—*benevolence*—to represent the action rather than the actor. In Johnson's time *benevolence* had the primary meaning we give it now ("Disposition to do good" is the way he puts it), but it also had the subsidiary meaning of a kind of tax, which had been devised by Edward IV and abolished by Richard III. *Benevolence*, in other words, has gone the opposite direction from its fellow philanthropic words: it once meant money and now means only love.

Charity, like *philanthropy*, is a word which used to point toward love and now points toward money. (Note that the Spanish and Italian word *caro* and its English equivalent *dear* still gesture simultaneously in both directions.) In Dr. Johnson's period the word teetered in the balance: Johnson's first three definitions of *charity* are all allied with the old meanings of *philanthropy* (goodwill, universal love, and so on), while definitions four and five ("liberality to the poor" and "alms") tend toward our modern interpretation of philanthropic activity. *Charity* in the singular can still occasionally retain a religious overtone, a sense of disinterested tenderness, but the plural form has been eaten up by the business of public giving. Roget's Thesaurus evades the problem by giving only the adjectival form, *charitable*, thus restricting the meaning to spiritual values (kind, generous, Christian, and so forth). Oddly enough, my 1958 edition of Roget, billed on the cover as "up-to-date" and "newly written," similarly restricts the meaning of philanthropy ("altruism, humanity . . . good will to men"); that is, this supposedly revised edition ignores the financial meanings that have seeped into the word since 1852, when Mr. Roget first published his listings. These meanings have by now so completely flooded the word *philanthropy* that it has for us an inherent tone of hypocrisy: its philology suggests a personally expressed love for humanity, but its present practice mainly involves relatively impersonal monuments to vast fortunes of celebrated donors. These days a philanthropist is much more likely to act out of desire for reflected self-love than out of a disinterested love of humankind. (Thoreau would have me question, though, the extent to which the word *disinterested* could ever apply to philanthropy, even in his day and earlier.)

———

Henry James wrote his final novel, *The Golden Bowl,* just as philanthropy was shifting from its largely attitudinal to its more financial connotation, and his philanthropist, Adam Verver, is parked squarely in the center of that shift. A "simple," "innocent" American businessman who has somehow managed to accumulate gigantic sums of money (James, no idiot, must have been aware of the irony), Verver goes around Europe collecting "fine" things—old, beautiful, artistic things—for a projected museum to be located in his rough American hometown (shades of J. P. Morgan). Two of the things he collects are an extremely handsome, nobly born Italian son-in-law and a young, beautiful American wife. Both of these purchases—Prince Amerigo and Charlotte—are well aware of the extent to which good money has been paid for them, and they feel correspondingly and somewhat oppressively obliged. The Prince becomes especially conscious of the unremittingness of his situation during a dinner party in which he occasionally catches his father-in-law's eye:

> This gaze rested at its ease, but it neither lingered nor penetrated, and was, to the Prince's fancy, much of the

THE AMATEUR

same order as any glance directed, for due attention, from the same quarter, to the figure of a check received in the course of business and about to be enclosed to a banker. It made sure of the amount—and just so, from time to time, the amount of the Prince was made sure. He was being thus, in renewed installments, perpetually paid in; he already reposed in the bank as a value, but subject, in this comfortable way, to repeated, to infinite endorsement.

Charlotte, always the quicker of the two to formulate things in words, has confided to the Prince, several pages earlier, a similar realization about her own situation:

"I've got so much, by my marriage"—for she had never for a moment concealed from him how "much" she felt it and was finding it—"that I should deserve no charity if I stinted my return. Not to do that, to give back on the contrary all one can, are just one's decency and one's honour and one's virtue. These things, henceforth, if you're interested to know, are my rule of life, the absolute little gods of my worship, the holy images set up on the wall. O yes, since I'm not a brute," she had wound up, "you shall see me as I *am!*" Which was therefore as he had seen her—dealing always, from month to month, from day to day and from one occasion to the other, with the duties of a remunerated office.

The language of James's paragraph encompasses all the different senses of philanthropy, even extending to the religious ("the absolute little gods"). And lest we forget that the "charity" Charlotte speaks of involves both love and money, we get James's constant reminder of the compression of the two, in the form of the Prince's frequent address to her, "*cara mia.*" Charlotte is both expensive and beloved—very "dear."

What is disturbing about *The Golden Bowl* (aside from all the other, perhaps more obviously anxiety-producing elements, like the love affair between Verver's son-in-law and Verver's wife) is the way the two kinds of philanthropy—love for the nearest representatives of humanity and gift-giving on a vast impersonal scale—both turn out to be riddled with ego. Verver's acquisitiveness seems appropriate on neither front: money seems a sufficient but not, finally, satisfactory way of acquiring either a spouse or an artistic heritage. Yet James doesn't let us rest with condemning Adam Verver. When you read *The Golden Bowl* you begin to feel that all love partakes of ownership and all philanthropy of self-glorification. The very possibility and even the value of "disinterestedness" come under fire, especially since the most disinterested character in the novel, Fanny Assingham, is the person largely responsible for landing her friends in their distressing situation. We come back in the end to a viewpoint very much like Thoreau's, but one in which the ante is greatly raised by the move from the isolation of a bean field to the necessarily complex relations of a social world. One can remain innocent of the failures and excesses of philanthropy only by remaining entirely apart from society, as Thoreau does; but James won't let his characters off that hook, and most of us can't get off it either.

———

These days very few of us encounter philanthropists in the flesh, except in the sense I began with, as small almsgivers. For the most part our experiences with modern philanthropy are experiences with philanthropic organizations. (The latest version of the OED reflects this transition by recording the word *philanthropoid*, first used in 1949 and defined as "a professional philanthropist, a worker for a charitable or grant-awarding institution.") As a consultant and a project director, I have been on both the giving and receiving ends of these transactions—have been, so to speak, both philanthropoid and philanthropee. Of the two, I found receiving far less painful.

I don't know what things were like in the salad days of organizational philanthropy (or even when those salad days might have been—I would guess the 1950s). But since 1981, when I entered the picture, philanthropy has become more and more of a business. A foundation may still be handing out "free" money, but it wants to make sure it's getting some kind of bang for its buck. It "evaluates" competing requests; it "measures benefit" (even, sometimes, on a crude cost-per-person basis); and it demands "accountability" from its recipients. These recipients, too, now tend to be organizations rather than individuals. Nobody, for instance, gives money directly to a poor person any more (except, under duress, on the street). Instead, a wealthy organization transfers funds to a "service" organization, which in turn sees that something is done for the poor. The process works similarly when the beneficiaries are medical, educational, arts, or environmental agencies rather than just organizations serving the poor: in such cases the philanthropic justification has to do with "improving the quality of life" rather than strictly spreading the wealth.

Severing the tie between the individual donor and the individual recipient has had both good and bad effects. On the negative side, there is something ludicrous, if not downright offensive, about having a group that serves meals to the homeless (or carries out some other obviously philanthropic service) fill out quarterly reports describing the cost-benefit ratio of the operation. This is *Hard Times* Gradgrindism at its worst. On the other hand, the presence of an intervening organization certainly reduces the degree of forelock-tugging required by the philanthropic relationship. If they don't directly confront their benefactors, the poor needn't act, or even feel, particularly grateful, and that itself is a great boon.

Ironically enough, philanthropy works best, in the

sense of being most painless and least embarrassing to the participating parties, in the area where it is least needed: that is, the arts. Over the years artists and philanthropies have tried to portray arts grants as in some way equivalent, if not identical in nature, to grants that benefit those in dire need. But the brute fact is that art doesn't *need* philanthropy. The artist, as a poverty-stricken consumptive, may need a handout; that's a different matter, and in that case he qualifies as a poor person, not as an artist. But art itself is something that will either generate and survive or not, regardless of foundation grants. It may be a lot easier for people to *see* the art if philanthropies support art museums and symphony orchestras and theater companies and literary magazines; but that support will not in itself guarantee the production of good art. I'm not saying that artists don't work for money: *Great Expectations* and *The Golden Bowl* might never have been produced if their authors hadn't been able to make a living as writers. But I sincerely doubt that a nineteenth-century MacArthur award, if granted to either Dickens or James, would have led to anything greater than those two novels. The rallying cry of most foundations is that they want to "make a difference"; but in the area of the arts, the flat truth is that they often don't.

Philanthropic organizations have a sneaking suspicion of this fact. In order to squelch the uncomfortable realization, they often tack on some requirement for

"public benefit" in their grants to artists: the writer must
give a reading at a public school, the dancer must perform in a women's prison, and so forth. These requirements imply a belief that pure support of art is not an
appropriate function of philanthropy. Such rules also
suggest that the artist is somehow outside the bounds of
public obligation, and needs to be brought into the fold.
But the "public benefit" clause is a foolish way to do this,
for the artist—if he can be compromised at all—will
already have been compromised by the mere acceptance
of the philanthropist's money. That, rather than any spu-
rious public appearances, is what marks his signature on
the social contract. Like Pip taking the convict's money,
the artist irreversibly acknowledges his bond with society simply by accepting the grant. Depending on his personality, he will then proceed to honor the bond or bite
the hand that feeds him. Neither response will determine
the quality of the art he produces, and neither will ultimately be caused by his having been given a grant. The
renegade artist will be a renegade with or without philanthropic support, and the conformist will be likewise.

On some level artists suspect all this, which is why
they are so irritating for foundation people to deal with.
They accept philanthropic support as their unnecessary
but nonetheless demanded due; they feel the philanthropies should be grateful for the opportunity to assist
them. In this belief history supports them: we can now
see that Leonardo da Vinci's and Michelangelo's patrons

got a lot more from their artists, in terms of public recognition and spiritual glorification, than those artists ever took from them. And, as James suggested, more recent philanthropists like the fictional Adam Verver and the very real J. P. Morgan actually collected art for the fun of it—to redound to their own material and aesthetic credit—rather than out of the kind of self-sacrificing "love of mankind" that motivated do-gooders like Jane Addams.

Because there is no real bond of obligation or gratitude incurred on either side, philanthropy to the arts is somehow cleaner and clearer than other kinds of giving. This is not at all to say that it is better: I would be sorry indeed if my words were used as an excuse to transfer millions of dollars from Head Start programs and Meals-on-Wheels to the coffers of art museums and opera companies. But giving to the arts lacks some of the inherent inconsistencies that Thoreau discerned in philanthropy. Arts giving, unlike other kinds, doesn't inevitably set up a high/low status relationship between the two participants in the event. And arts giving, because it really doesn't involve a felt response to human need, cleanly severs the bond between philanthropy and its Greek roots. This kind of giving isn't about love; it's purely about money. That may sound brutal, but it is in fact less disturbing than the curious mixture that remains in the other philanthropic fields.

Back in the Reagan/Bush era, there was a television

commercial for United Way that took various forms, each one showing some grateful recipient of United Way funds acting in a heartwarming manner. At the end of the commercial the recipient would look out at the anonymous TV audience and say, "I don't know you, but I love you." This is the opposite of the clean break: this is the "phil" in philanthropy taken literally, but with the direction of the love reversed. Here it's the receiver, and not the giver, who feels impersonal love of his fellow man. And the love is not a disinterested feeling, but a coerced and coercive combination of gratitude and pleading. "Thanks for helping me, and could you please help me some more?" is what that commercial really meant. If that is love, then my tortured giving-up of a few coins to a street person is generosity.

OUT OF ACADEMIA

F or much of the 1980s I wavered among three possible careers. One was the job I happened to be doing at the time to bring in the bulk of my income: consulting to nonprofit organizations, primarily to foundations. Though this work was relatively lucrative (relative to the other two careers, I mean), my distaste for bureaucratic paperwork, arm's-length administration, and the general office environment made it unlikely that I would stick to it for very long. The second career was that of writer and editor—a job I was effectively doing full time from 1980 onward, but one that produced a negative cash flow until at least 1990. (And even when the cash flow was positive, it wasn't *very* positive. I remember going to the dentist in 1987, shortly after my first book was published, and having the hygienist chattily say, "So I gather you've sold a book since you were last here!" I informed her, through a mouthful of fingers, that "sold" was hardly the appropriate verb for the amount of money that had changed hands in the transaction.) The third career was academia.

Graduate school in English, at least during the time I attended, was the sort of thing you could pursue in the interstices of the rest of your life. Once you had finished your coursework—which at Berkeley took only two years, or at most three—you did not have to remain fully enrolled in the university while you were working on your doctoral dissertation. Given the length of time that most people spent working on their dissertations (and, within that period, the amount of time they spent *not* working on their dissertations), it was difficult to differentiate between people who had actually quit the Ph.D. program and people who were just taking a while finishing. In fact, one never knew for sure which of the two categories one belonged to until one finished the dissertation; those who never finished remained in a permanent state of definitional flux.

I finished my dissertation after seven years in the program—not a speed record for completion, but not an embarrassment either. (My thesis, for the record, was entitled "The Urban Tradition: Transformations of London as Reflected in Dickens, James, and Conrad." The colon and the passive voice are especially typical of the genre.) Finishing the dissertation was made simpler by the fact that I had long since come to view the Ph.D. thesis as just another writing job, one that needed to be submitted to three clients for approval before I could be paid with my degree. I was implicitly aided in this approach by my dissertation director, a then-young academic who has since gone on to help found a school of literary theory known as Pragmatism. Exercising an embryonic version of this philosophy, he said about the dissertation draft I had recently given him: "Well, if you just want a Ph.D., I'll sign right now. But if you want a job at a place like Hopkins or Yale, there are a few little rewrites you'll have to do."

"Sign right now," I promptly answered, leaning across his desk to indicate with my index finger the appropriate place on the degree-granting form.

(Earlier there had been another ticklish moment when I showed a draft of the first few chapters to my friend and former teacher Christopher Ricks. Christopher, with his usual acuity, pointed out that there was a conceptual problem at the core of my project: whereas I could prove that the city of London had indeed altered over the given fifty-year period, and could also mark differences in style as I moved from Dickens to James to Conrad, I hadn't actually demonstrated any causal link between the two. "*I* know that, and *you* know that, but let's keep it under our hats, shall we?" I said. And he did, bless him, though he believes in perfectionism on all fronts, while I limit mine to the places where it will show.)

No doubt my attitude toward correcting the shortcomings of my thesis illustrates how poorly suited I was to an academic career. I did not interpret it that way, though. I simply knew that I did not *want* a job at Hopkins or Yale, because taking such a job would require moving away from Berkeley. I had already met the man I was to marry; I'd been supporting myself for years; *The Threepenny Review* was just getting on its feet. In short, I had a life. Why should I give it up for an academic career? I did deign to apply for the single Bay Area job available that year, at Stanford University, but Stanford did not deign to hire me.

In subsequent years, when the foundation world seemed too oppressive to be borne, I undertook several semesters of visiting lectureships at UC Santa Cruz. I loved constructing the reading lists for my classes— it was wonderful to be thinking and talking about nineteenth-century literature again—but in the course of teaching those books to undergraduates I discovered several things about myself. One was that I hated grading papers. It was bad enough, I felt, to read an inept poem or a boring short story that someone had been passionately inspired to write, the sort of reading I did all the time in my *Threepenny* work; but to read a poorly constructed paper that someone had been *forced* to write seemed meaninglessly painful. I also learned that I was hapless at dealing with the politics of an English department (or even of a "Lit Board," as it is euphemistically called at Santa Cruz); I made enemies right and left, and wanted to kill most of my colleagues. But the worst thing I discovered about myself was that I am not a very good teacher. I am lively and enthusiastic in talking about books I love, so I am a good-enough teacher for students who are already interested in the material; but for the students who really need to be taught and helped, I am hopeless. And if you can't teach those students, you don't belong in teaching.

I allowed myself to drift away from academic employment. Luckily this drift occurred at around the time that *Threepenny* began paying me a small salary, so I didn't starve. This decision to leave the university world was never a fully conscious one, and it always seemed as if it might someday be reversed. So it was with a great deal of surprise, some chagrin, and an unforgivable trace of pride that I read in a recent *TLS* review: "Having turned her back on academia . . . Lesser has taken her magazine in the same direction." *I* turned *my* back? And all those years I had thought academia was turning *its* back on *me*.

This is disingenuous, and a little false. Nobody really did any backturning. When I speak of myself as being "out of" academia, I use the phrase in part the way racetrack commentators use it, to cite the heritage of a particular horse by noting that she is "by" Thunderbird and "out of" Flying Lady. Academia is my dam, you might say, contributing half the genetic stew that went into the training of my adult mind. From the university and its scholars I acquired my respect for close reading as an analytic technique, my belief in the serious importance of literature, and my admiration for impractical thought as a necessary and beautiful intellectual activity. I still enjoy academic talk, and I count among my friends a disproportionate number of my former teachers, including one who eventually married my friend Katharine, another with whom I have lunch every week, and a third who came up with the title for my last book.

So why, if I feel such affection for its denizens, did I get out of academia? External circumstances played a part, of course, but in my experience such circumstances, when you give in to them, always prove to be internal as well. Finally, if I had to give a single reason, I would say I wasn't suited to the academy because I wanted to exercise a kind of judgment that was not normal there. If you are an old-fashioned literary scholar, you are presented with a collection of excellent books to work on, and you practice your techniques on this already certified group. Or, if you are a newfangled literary scholar, you find a collection of writing that fits the category you want to study, and you don't care whether the books are good or bad, or even whether they're books; you are only interested in the patterns you can discern. In either case evaluation is irrelevant. But evaluation is central to what I do—not even what I *want* to do, since that implies choice, but what I *need* to do.

And this need, I began to discover, extended beyond literature to the other arts: to film, to painting, to theater, to dance, even to opera (which is the rich godmother of all the arts) and television (which is their poor cousin). There didn't seem to be room in academia for this kind of relatively untutored omnivorousness. Increasingly I found myself focusing on the experience that takes place when a reader or observer or auditor encounters a work of art: that meeting place between one person's sensibility and another person's creation. Inevitably, that sensibility was going to be mine—since, as a critic, I had no true access to anyone else's—but if the focus was necessarily narrow and inward-looking in this one respect, I wanted it to be as broad and outward-facing as possible in other ways. I didn't want to have arbitrary lines drawn between things: between old masterpieces and contemporary works, between art and the rest of the world, between criticism and conversation. I wanted the whole terrain. And, in my own tiny way, I got it.

DANCE LESSONS

R ecently I had occasion to spend the evening dancing, to the music of a not fully professional but nonetheless adequate salsa band, in the company of several old friends. Most of these friends were writers, and in the manner of writers we had spent countless hours talking, eating, and drinking together, but rarely, if ever, dancing. After a few numbers had been played (during which my husband and I had eagerly taken to the dance floor), one of my old friends—a man prone to beautifully crafted, restrained writing and profusely exaggerated speech—came up to me and said, "You're *good*! You can *really* dance! You should be doing that for a *living*! Why are you wasting your time with *words* when you can do *that*?"

He was, in many ways, wrong. I am not good enough, and have never been close to good enough, to dance professionally. In my lifetime, I have been a beginner in many different dance forms. At various times I have taken modern dance (of the Martha Graham, Mary Wigman, and

José Limón varieties), jazz dance, ballet, Afro-Haitian dance, salsa, Balkan folk dance, Israeli folk dance, and yoga movement. In each case I began very promisingly and then reached a plateau beyond which I could not progress. (Generally, but not always, it had to do with turns.) Other people who initially seemed less talented moved ahead of me, and soon I was left in the dust. A girl from my childhood ballet classes went on to become a professional ballerina in Europe. Several women from my college modern dance classes are pursuing careers as dancers in New York. I, on the other hand, am stuck with words, earthbound.

Yet dance is, and always was, very important to me. In this way, I see what my writer friend means. If you *could* do that, how could you bear not to? Dancing is the closest thing I have ever felt to flying. I don't mean flying in an airplane, which is basically like riding in a bus or a train; I mean lifting yourself off the ground with the power of your own wings, as you do in dreams. Dance allows you to feel as if you're conquering physical laws, especially in those supreme moments when you sense the congruence of the music and your own motion, when the swell of the rhythm seems to lift your body off the ground. Surfers must feel like this, I imagine, and ski jumpers—perhaps great athletes of any kind. As an essentially unathletic person, I have only felt it through dance.

My husband also loves to dance, and dance has meant

a great deal in his life, too. (But that is *his* tale, and I won't go into it here.) We fell in love without knowing this about each other, but there must have been some secret signal we were sending, unbeknownst to ourselves. Certainly other people have picked it up. "You seem like people who would go out dancing together," said a then-new friend who met us before we were married. And when we were younger we did go out dancing a lot. Then we stopped for a while, because every evening on the dance floor led to a giant fight. It was as if things we didn't want to acknowledge about each other, hidden sources of conflict and animosity, inescapably emerged when we were dancing. Lately, though, we have been able to dance together again; perhaps, after twenty years, we are beginning to find those secret differences less frightening.

Because we both felt strongly about dance, we sent our son to all sorts of dance and movement classes—with his willing consent, I should add. By the time he was seven he had taken ballet, Afro-American jazz, gymnastics, tae kwon do, and capoeira. (These last two are technically martial art forms—from Korea and Brazil, respectively—but they use a number of dancelike motions.) My East Coast friends felt this was very California of us, to be sending our child to all these weird classes.

And perhaps it was. There does seem to be some connection between California and dance. This link is partly historical and biographical, in that European modern dancers fleeing the Second World War seemed to settle in disproportionately large numbers in California (just as their counterparts in music and drama, for more obvious reasons, tended to relocate to Los Angeles). My childhood modern dance teacher was a German refugee, and so was the founding figure of Stanford's modern dance program. But there's also a climate here that produces home-grown dance and dancers. Performers from Martha Graham to Allegra Kent to Twyla Tharp all hail from California. (That they had to go east to find work is another story.) And bizarre offshoots of dance, ranging from the tree-hugging, self-expressive, improvisation-based therapies to the chanting, swaying, chime-ringing performances of the Hare Krishnas, have also found fertile soil here.

I hate improvisation myself, and whenever a dance class turns in that direction I know it's time for me to leave. It's not that I don't like to move freely in time to music. I do that, after all, every time I dance at a party, and I often do it alone in the comfort of my living room. But on both these sorts of occasion the act of making up my steps is safely private—in the former case because it is shielded by the social nature of the event (I am, that is, operating within the relatively strict conventions of a dance party) and in the latter case because no one else is there. What I hate about "guided" improvisation, of the kind you are asked to do in some modern dance classes, is that you are essentially being commanded to bare your soul. It's like making a confession over a public address system, or having one of your dreams projected onto a movie screen. If you take the endeavor seriously, you are going to reveal extremely personal things (or, at least, imagine you are revealing them) to people you hardly know. A dance class, for me, is a place to be somewhat anonymous; I don't want my interior life splayed out in front of the other participants, except insofar as it happens to be revealed by the way I do the pre-set steps. Or perhaps I feel that to dance *at all* is to reveal oneself, almost to the verge of embarrassment, so that the additional dragging-in of one's inner life is bound to tip fruitful nervousness over into paralyzing shame.

Dance, for me, is peculiarly interior in another way as well. It goes straight to the ganglia, bypassing the cerebrum. There are ways in which this is not entirely true: one has to think hard to make or follow patterns, and the most brilliant choreographers are, in my experience, among the fastest thinkers. But to the extent it *is* true, it is true of watching dance as well as doing it. That is, seeing a beautiful dance gesture moves me on a physical level, before I even have a chance to understand *why* I find it beautiful. The pleasure of watching Baryshnikov leap (in his prime), or Savion Glover levitate over his tap shoes, or Mark Morris dance in *The Office*, or Gene Kelly perform with cartoon characters, is something that seems to originate inside my rib cage rather than in my brain. When I see John Travolta execute a few dance steps in *Pulp Fiction*, I don't think, "Oh, how clever of Quentin Tarantino to echo *Saturday Night Fever*." I think, "Oh! How beautifully he moves!" The appreciation is entirely visceral at first, and only subsequently intellectual.

I have tried to hold on to something of this feeling in my writing about dance. I am not primarily, or even often, a dance critic, but my engagement with the form occasionally draws me into writing about it, and those essays seem, in retrospect, to have more of me in them than most of my other critical writing. Is this because I am writing about bodies rather than words? I strongly doubt it, since anything, even bodies—*especially* bodies, these days—can be made grist for the abstract, academic mill. Is it, then, because I love good dance so much, and hate bad dance with an equal if opposite passion? But I feel the same way about good and bad books. Or is it, perhaps, that the effort to retain one's sense of that first visceral response, that pre-intellectual delight, is so comparatively easy with dance? I can think about a performance and make up theories to my heart's content without in any way damaging or erasing my initial feeling of wonder. The pleasure is still there, long after the dance is over.

PASSIONATE WITNESS

I began following the Mark Morris Dance Group in 1990, when I arranged a trip to New York specifically to see them perform at the Brooklyn Academy of Music. I had heard a lot about the company from friends, so I expected to like what I saw. But I did not expect to be completely smitten—to spend the rest of my New York visit urging everyone I knew to get out to BAM, telling them that I had finally seen a great artwork, a masterpiece, made in my lifetime.

The piece I saw that first time—the evening-length *L'Allegro, il Penseroso, ed il Moderato*—remains, for me, an exemplary high point. Choreographed to a Handel piece which itself was composed as the setting for poems by Milton, *L'Allegro* displays many of Mark Morris's virtues and virtuosities. It is at once rooted in history and strikingly contemporary. The line back to the seventeenth-century words and the eighteenth-century music feels strong and unbroken, and yet the dancers are performing steps and combinations that seem thoroughly modern. Mimetic gestures of book-reading, bird-singing, game-hunting—gestures which evoke the pastoral scenes on medieval tapestries—combine with the vigorous rhythms and patterns of Eastern European circle dances. Archaic courtliness intertwines with humorous inventiveness, as a female soloist's graceful adagio emerges from a full-group rendering of arm-shaking, leg-swinging mirth. Men and women share and exchange roles, with one ensemble dance having the women lift the men, followed by the men lifting the women. (It is part of Morris's acute intelligence as a choreographer—a social as well as aesthetic intelligence—that he thought to have the lifts performed in this order. Had the men lifted the women first, the women's lifts would have seemed a mere joke on traditional techniques. Coming first, they have a tenderness, a maternal protectiveness that is all their own; only secondarily do they become part of the joke about relative sex roles that is indeed being made. The pairing, in this order, evokes a moving revelation rather than a guffaw.)

Mark Morris himself does not dance in *L'Allegro*, so the first time I ever saw him was when he came out at the end to take his curtain call. Morris's curtain calls are an art form in themselves—I have come to be quite a connoisseur of them, in the years since—but I didn't realize that then. All I knew was that I couldn't take my eyes off this tall, slightly bulky, curly-maned, weirdly beautiful, absolutely commanding figure. (The next day, watching him perform in a mixed program with Mikhail Baryshnikov, I had the same experience, to my even greater surprise: I had never before seen anybody who could draw my eye away from Baryshnikov.) Standing to applaud at the end of *L'Allegro*, surrounded by the rest of the clapping, screaming BAM audience, I felt the charge of the choreographer's presence as if it were a blast of electricity. "He's like a rock star!" I said to my friend Mindy, a dance critic who had brought me to the performance.

Later, as we were climbing into our taxi in front of the auditorium, I saw Morris emerge from the building with a small group of people—heading out for a late dinner, perhaps. When they passed near us, I stuck my head out the taxi window and yelled at him, "You're great! It was great!" He turned toward me and beamed an angelic "Thanks!" Hiding within the taxi, torn between her embarrassment at my outburst and her pleasure at my enthusiasm, Mindy wryly pointed out to me that the name of the cab company, which was emblazoned on the side of the car facing Morris, was "CHEERS."

I knew nothing of Mark Morris's history at the time, but I subsequently learned that this particular production was something of a watershed in his career. Before *L'Allegro* he was widely viewed as the bad boy of modern dance. "Boy" can be taken almost literally here: he was twenty-four when he founded his own company, and all of thirty-two when he choreographed *L'Allegro* in 1988. *Lovey*, Morris's 1985 dance set to music by the Violent Femmes, has the dancers, who are dressed in shabby underwear and nightclothes, miming sex acts with little naked dolls. As the choreographer of John Adams's opera *Nixon in China* and the director of dance for the Théâtre Royal de la Monnaie in Brussels, Morris was famous for spitting in the face of bourgeois audiences, for taking previously inoffensive art forms and lending them an earthy, streetwise capacity to offend. This reputation does some violence to the truth, for all of Mark Morris's work is in some way respectful (to its musical sources, at the very least) and none of it has the irritating "Gotcha!" quality that one finds in the work of artists who have one eye cocked on audience reaction. Nor was *L'Allegro* Morris's first satisfyingly beautiful piece—though it remains, I think, his most satisfyingly beautiful piece to date.

I am using the term "satisfyingly beautiful" in a very specific sense, a sense that's been suggested to me by the choreography of Mark Morris. From what I have seen of his dances (and I've seen less than a third of his hundred or so pieces—some, alas, only on videotape), I conclude that Morris is after two very distinct effects. One of these has to do with asking a question, testing out a theory, opening up an area of inquiry; the other has to with providing a worked-out, completed (if only temporarily

173

final) answer. In the first category I would put such dances as *Ten Suggestions* (which he originally choreographed in 1981, to piano music by Tcherepnin) and *Three Preludes* (made, to Gershwin's music, in 1992). Each of these pieces carries its tentativeness in its title; each, as it happens, is a solo in which Morris has alternated with Baryshnikov. In such works he seems to be trying out certain ideas about dance and about life. What difference does it make to have the same gestures performed by two very different bodies? How can casualness combine with precision? How can props be used? (*Ten Suggestions* features a hula hoop.) How do hands dance, as well as, or in contrast to, feet? How is stillness a kind of dancing? How can we keep a dance in our mind once the dancer has disappeared? Where do dances come from, and where do they go? You can watch these two pieces over and over again, with Morris or Baryshnikov, on stage or on tape, and still feel that, however much you discover each time, their essence has escaped you. Their only graspable point is that they cannot be grasped. They experiment with and comment on the ephemerality of dance.

And then there are the other Mark Morris dances, the ones that seem to hand you a full goblet and allow you to carry it, ever so carefully, away. These pieces from which you can drink your fill include *Dido and Aeneas*, his evening-long work to Purcell's opera, in which Morris himself plays both Dido and the Sorceress. But the dance needn't be long to be complete. *Gloria*, an early work to Vivaldi, has this quality; so does the 1992 *Beautiful Day*, to a cantata that may be by Bach. Nor need such a dance be set to classical music: *Lovey* seems to me to be one of the filling, satisfying pieces, though the beauty with which it satisfies is a fierce, antagonistic, frightening kind, not at all like the welcoming beauty of *L'Allegro*.

There does seem to be a connection, though, between Morris's use of vocal music and the kind of satisfaction I'm referring to. His questioning, what-if, how-does pieces are all set to purely instrumental music—or, in the case of the 1990 *Behemoth*, to no music at all. In the vocal pieces, the words are not just there to provide plot (a device which we sometimes confuse with satisfaction or completion), for a Mark Morris dance can include elements of plot and still be both wordless and open-ended—as is *Wonderland*, for instance, the 1989 dance-noir set to Schoenberg. No, the importance of vocal music appears to be that through it, in combination with dance, Morris can engage the whole body. The satisfying beauty of a piece like *L'Allegro* comes from the sense that everything which can possibly be used *has* been used— that the world, at least for a brief moment at the end of the dance, has no inexhausted possibilities.

If this makes satisfaction sound like death, it may help explain why Morris feels the need to keep making the open-ended kind of work. To obtain a sense of completion is not the only desirable end of dance, for either its viewers or its makers. We want to feel at times that things remain unanswered; we want to sense the lure of the ungraspable and be reassured by the possibility of change. The ephemerality of dance is not just its tragedy. It is also its blessing, for it connects dance with our lives, whose completeness is not a quality we either can or wish to see.

With his particular form of choreographic genius, Mark Morris has managed to incorporate some of this changeability, this lifelikeness, even into a completely satisfying work like *L'Allegro, il Penseroso, ed il Moderato.* Departing from both Milton (who ended with Melancholy) and Handel (who, in typical eighteenth-century mode, ended with Moderation), Morris begins *and* ends the piece with Happiness. That is, he turns Milton's and Handel's linear structure into a circle—just as he does in the final moments of the dance itself, which ends as a large, fast, joyous circle dance culminating in a single moment of upward-reaching stillness. The many dancers have become a single motion, and unity has been imposed on division, but not by arriving at a logical and irrefutable compromise. Morris has simply chosen—arbitrarily, personally, and whimsically—to end on a note of happiness. Nothing in either the world or this work of art leads you to conclude that happiness is a necessary or permanent outcome; and yet the moment feels right, and final, and true.

Part of what makes it feel final and true is that, like any moment in dance, the ending of *L'Allegro* is only temporary and contingent. This is one of the things dance and its ephemerality can teach us; this is one of the things Morris has taught himself through his experiments, his "suggestions" and "preludes." When one gets to the end of the music, one must choose an end to the dance, but that end is not a permanent stoppage, not a closure for all time. It is an end only to that particular piece, and in another work, under other circumstances, the choreographer might just as arbitrarily and personally choose the opposite course.

———

When you attach yourself to a cherished artist, as I have attached myself to Mark Morris, you cede to that artist a certain portion of your own intellectual development. You are not just the learned critic, commenting on the work; you are also the novice, being molded by that work. In such cases you sometimes have to trust the artist more than you trust yourself. He (or she—but for me such artists are almost always "he") may be working a few steps ahead of you, and you may not be ready to absorb what he has made. Sometimes the new piece itself will teach you things you need to know to respond to it, but that process can take years, and your first impulse may be to resist the new direction because it is not exactly what your beloved artist has done before.

I think it is useful for critics, especially extremely opinionated critics, to have a few touchstone artists of this sort. I have several myself; in addition to Mark Morris my list includes the filmmaker Errol Morris (no relation), the novelist Ian McEwan, and the poet Thom Gunn. The point is not that I respond with equal enthusiasm to everything they do. I don't turn into brainless, appreciative mush; I must still keep my wits about me, and my own tastes. But I do give them the benefit of the doubt in a way that I am rarely able to do with other artists. If I don't like something in a Mark Morris dance, I will ask myself whether I am wrong to feel that way. I will see the dance over and over, if I can, and I will keep asking myself this question. Sometimes I come out on my side; less often I come out on his. But either way, the process of thinking about what he has done and why he has done it alters me as a critic.

An artist with a strong personality, like a critic with a strong personality, is always at risk of seeing things too much his own way. He needs to rely on his own judgments, but he must also temper those judgments by recognizing the needs and capacities of the people around him. If he is a choreographer, he will necessarily shape the dancers who work with him; and if he is a good choreographer, he will also be shaped *by* them. One of the things I appreciated the very first time I saw the Mark Morris company was the individuality of the dancers' styles. Varying as they do in shape, age, sex, weight, height, race, nationality, and background, they could hardly convey a chorus-line rigidity of style. But their variety goes beyond superficial appearance. What Morris's choreography does is to allow his dancers to express their own distinct personalities even as they are dancing his steps.

And yet, there is a kind of unity to their effort. This is not just the unity of their impressive musicality (though here they triumph over any other company of dancers I have ever seen: *no one* misses the beat), but a stronger and deeper sense of coherence. When I saw *L'Allegro* I had not yet seen Mark Morris dance, but I knew what he must be like as a dancer. I saw it in the precise delicacy of Keith Sabado's movements, and in the way he used his face as a beacon from the stage to the audience. I saw it in the relaxed looseness of Guillermo Resto's shoulders and arms, the strength of his torso and legs, the way dancing seemed for him both casual and intense. I saw it in the sprightly enthusiasm of June Omura, the gentle melancholy of Ruth Davidson, the quivering wit of Kraig Patterson, the elegant ease of Penny Hutchinson. I saw bits and pieces of Mark Morris in all his dancers' styles, individual and singular though they were—so that the next day, when I saw Morris himself perform, he was utterly recognizable, almost familiar. And something in his choreography was also recognizable to me, as if I had seen it before in dreams, or had been waiting a lifetime, expectantly, to see it.

I am roughly the same age as Mark Morris—to be exact, I am four years older—and, like Morris, I was obsessed by Balkan folk dancing in my teens. (I took longer to outgrow it than Morris did: I was still performing with a Balkan dance group during college. But then he had other kinds of dance to move on to.) When I hear people talk about the influence of Balkan dance on Morris's work, I want to say, "Yes, but . . ." Yes, it was a search for roots and community in the Sixties and early Seventies. Yes, it was a way of bringing together song and dance, audience and participant, couple and group, tradition and novelty. But it was darker, more divisive, more interesting things as well. It was getting out of the house when you were a teenager, escaping from your own family into some other, less personal simulacrum of a family. It was excitement, and late nights, and parties after the parties. It was the lure of sex and the safety of displacement. It was getting to dance without being asked, evading the teenage hell of sock hops and cheerleaders, exerting a more adult kind of attraction on people older than yourself. It was a realm of dance in which skill still mattered, in which you couldn't just get up and wiggle (as any fool could do during Sixties happenings and rock concerts) but had to master the steps, acquire a style, become a *dancer*. It was precision in a world of sloppiness, and "heightened awareness" of a predictable, self-induced, un-drug-related variety. It was a place in which everyone was accepted, but in which discriminations (of grace, skill, knowledge) nonetheless mattered. It was a kind of community that was ideal for someone who was essentially, secretly solitary.

Morris's adulatory critics, Morris's dancers, and even, in some interviews, Morris himself repeatedly emphasize the role of "community" in his artworks and his artistic life. It is true that Mark Morris favors the ensemble dance and even the trio over the duet in his choreography. It is true that some of his dancers have been with him for nearly twenty years, and that many of them go out drinking and partying with him after rehearsals, night after night. There is, indeed, a sense of the group in his life and in his art. But there is also, just as strongly, a sense of the solitary, individual artist leaving his own personal signature on the world. To view Mark Morris as a product of the Sixties, complete with commune-like dance group, is utterly to misread what he is doing. At the core of Morris's work is allegiance to something other than the group—something I can only characterize with the inadequate words "artistic truth."

Such a sensibility is both omnivorous and highly discriminating. When he uses Indian ragas or Texas country music as the settings for his dances, Morris is not just being cute or fashionable: he is selecting the piece of music that, of all the music in the world, best suits his needs at the moment. People praise (or, less frequently, condemn) Mark Morris for fluttering between high art and low, for crossing boundaries between Western and Eastern music and dance, for being "multicultural" and "populist." But none of these distinctions has any meaning for Morris. He takes what he needs, wherever it comes from. He may be broad-minded, but he is also a snob. He wants only the best: the best dancers, the best music, the best performance of that music, the best literary texts, the best visual inspirations (for *L'Allegro* he used Blake's illustrations of Milton to shape several significant gestures), the best lighting and set design. He deeply believes in the concept of "the good," "the best"— he would not be able to work without it—and this very belief distinguishes him from the vast majority of iconoclastic artists who are wrongly grouped with him.

If I have made him sound arrogant, so be it—it is an arrogance that serves us well. If it were not for Mark Morris's arrogance (one might as easily call it "strength of mind" or "refusal to compromise"), he would not be able to function so resolutely as the conduit between his artistic vision and his audience. His dancers may continually have to submit themselves to his direction, but that is only a more tangible version of the submission he himself endures, to his own artistic imperatives. Morris the artist, not Morris the person, is the controlling force.

And yet (with Morris there is always an "and yet") the idea of a controlling force, true as it is to Morris's strength, is false to the freedom and individuality we can see in his work—not only in the dances but in the dancers themselves, with their unique and engaging styles. If he is a controlling force, it is in the same sense that gravity is: enormously powerful, but leaving one free to move, and in fact enabling one to dance. And, like gravity, Morris is there even when we don't see him, in every lift and fall of *L'Allegro*.

The gift Mark Morris gives us cannot be a permanent one. No choreographer's can. Without Morris to supervise every rehearsal, train every dancer, adjust every gesture, his dances would soon fade away, be travestied, cease to be themselves. The sense of completion they give us is an illusion. The sense of fulfillment, however, is not. Dance disappears, but the feeling it creates is left in the mind of the audience. We are its beneficiaries and its repositories. Years ago, witnessing for the first time this marvelous company and its marvelous work, I was grateful to be alive at the moment in history when Mark Morris was making his dances. And that feeling is with me still.

PORTRAIT OF A BALLERINA

———

A t a certain period, probably as the result of writing about Degas, I became interested in the connections between photography and dance—the meeting point, you might say, between stillness and movement. And sometime during that period I was sent a picture of a ballerina taken by George Platt Lynes. "George Lynes' pictures will contain, as far as I am concerned, all that will be remembered of my own repertory in a hundred years," George Balanchine had said in 1956. I took this as an exaggeration, an excessively dire prediction. But I could see, even in the single Lynes photograph I now had in my possession, exactly what it was that made Balanchine say this.

In this mesmerizing photo, the dancer leans in an unnaturally theatrical way on what is clearly a stage set, as if to depict with ironic mockery the idea of a "casual" pose. Her gaze, reinforcing the double message, is both cool and seductive. The beautiful young ballerina is

185

severely off-center, her right foot far forward in an an-
gled fourth position, her left invisible, so that she seems
to have no source of support. Or rather, she seems supported only by the single point—the meeting point of her
back and arm, the balletically crucial shoulderblade—at
which she delicately leans against the sharp edge of the
geometrically precise set. As in so much of Balanchine's
choreography, she appears to be balanced in a way that
taunts gravity.

While her body must obviously be working hard to
maintain its tilted verticality, her face and arms express
relaxation. Her lifted brows and sultry eyelids mirror the
cupid's-bow of her mouth, just as the crisscrossed span-
gles on her black dress mirror the pattern of her fishnet
tights. She is the picture of coherent, artificially manipulated composition, from coiffed head to elongated toe.
And yet there is a further element in the photograph that
contradicts all the signals about control, coherence, balance, precision. Swirling in the shadows that surround
the ballerina, bouncing with distracting intensity off the
metallic trim on her dress, playing around her bodice and
fluttering on her inner arms, are wild, free, unconfined
spots of brightness. This is, among other things, a photograph of dancing light.

"They contain something of the secret and seldom
realized intention of choreography," Balanchine said of
Lynes's pictures. Just as a choreographer focuses on

186

and responds to the human figure, so did George Platt Lynes: it was his central subject, whether in his portraits of Gertrude Stein, André Gide, Jean Cocteau, and other Paris artists of the 1920s, or his male nudes of the 1930s, or the oddly romantic, narrative self-portraits he did in the 1940s. After his initial burst of fame and success in the 1930s, his reputation peaked quickly. It was Hollywood which, according to Cecil Beaton, "killed" Lynes as a photographer in the late 1940s; the man himself died of cancer, at the age of forty-eight, in 1955. But his importance never faded among those who had admired his work, and his prints still sell to collectors and fans.

In March 1994 the Paul Kopeikin Gallery in Los Angeles organized a major retrospective of the work of George Platt Lynes, including the 1930s photo of the Balanchine ballerina. The ballerina herself was living, at the time, less than twenty miles from the Kopeikin Gallery, though she was unaware of the show that contained her portrait. Tamara Toumanova had been a permanent resident of Los Angeles since 1942, when she signed an RKO movie contract. Before that she danced in the Ballets Russes de Monte-Carlo in Paris, having been discovered by Balanchine at the age of eleven. In 1932 and 1933 she was one of his "baby ballerinas," dancing the lead roles in ballets he choreographed for her (*Cotillon, Le Bourgeois Gentilhomme, Mozartiana*, among others) before she was even a teenager. She stopped dancing for Balanchine sometime in the 1940s, but her connection to him lasted until his death; he would see her every time he brought his company to Los Angeles, often visiting her in her own home.

"Balanchine was close not only to me but to my family," Toumanova writes in her segment of *I Remember Balanchine*, and goes on to explain this by describing her emigré history—the aristocratic mother who had always loved ballet and who wanted more than anything else for her daughter to become a great ballerina; the engineer father, a colonel in the tsar's army, who received fourteen battle wounds over the course of his military career; the family's flight, following the Russian Revolution, from St. Petersburg to Vladivostok to Shanghai, where the father worked briefly as an engineer; and finally the decision to give up everything else and move to Paris so that Tamara could begin studying ballet at the age of five. Few maternal gambles can have paid off so handsomely.

———

Two months after the Kopeikin Gallery show, I pay a single visit to Toumanova at her Spanish-style bungalow on a quiet residential street in Beverly Hills. Filigree ironwork covers the front windows in Gothic arches; shiny, dark-green rubber plants grow near the house. In marked contrast to the well-kept property around it, a 1954 Buick Roadmaster sits on four flat tires in the driveway, looking as if it hadn't been moved in at least twenty years.

As, in fact, it hasn't. Tamara Toumanova and her mother bought this house in the early 1970s after both their husbands had died, and the car has been there, driverless, ever since. Before that the family lived in a large house in Bel Air. Tamara's husband—a producer and screenwriter named Casey Robinson, whom she married in 1944—was the only non-Russian-speaker in the household, though according to his widow he "adored everything Russian." The bulk of Toumanova's career was handled by her mother, who did everything from sew costumes to advise on camera angles; but she allowed her daughter's husband a subsidiary role in the movie world, where he was to "carry on the tradition that I did not become a poopsie-woopsie actress," as Toumanova now puts it.

When she opens the door to me, I am first surprised by Toumanova's height—shorter than I am, which puts her at just over five feet. She is, of course, considerably older than the slip of a girl in the George Platt Lynes photo. Her once-slender body is hidden by a long-sleeved, calf-length black dress, and her long hair, which she wore loose as late as the 1980s, is now swept back in a chignon. But the hair, though gray-flecked, is still dark, and the aristocratically molded face is still recognizably Toumanova's, with those intense, dramatically widening eyes and that elegantly aquiline nose. Injured recently in an accident and temporarily walking with a cane, Toumanova no longer has a ballerina's grace—except in her hands, which flash expressively from one gesture to another, now with raised annunciatory fingers, now pressed flat against her chest. Balanchine is still alive in those hands.

She apologizes for closing the door rapidly behind me, which she does to keep in the three cats: Kiss-Kiss, Caruso, and a third she calls Pussycat ("I don't even know what his name is," she explains, as if the other two had introduced themselves to her). The foyer through which I enter and the front parlor into which she invites me both seem extremely Russian. Every flat surface, every square inch of wall space is covered with something dark and rich and old. A chandelier hangs in the hallway ("Usually when earthquake starts I hear the banging of the chandeliers," Toumanova remarks calmly), and at least four glass candelabra rest on tables and shelves in the parlor; nonetheless, the overall light is uncharacteristically dim for midsummer, midday Los Angeles.

As she excuses herself to get the coffee she has prepared for my visit, I peer through the gloom and discern a red-hued Turkish rug, a set of green-velvet-covered chairs and sofas, some intricate metalwork of undisclosed function, a half-size harp, an extensive collection of china and glass swans, a somewhat smaller collection of porcelain eggs, and an uncountable number of photographs, drawings, and paintings, almost all of them depicting Tamara Toumanova at some stage of her dance career.

She emerges from the kitchen, not at all disconcerted to catch me snooping. "Did you see Karajan? And Chagall? And Balanchine in Paris? And Cocteau?" Each name is punctuated by a gesture toward the appropriate photograph. "Jean Cocteau was a very dear friend. This is Cocteau three weeks before he died. I have also the last letter he wrote; it was to me. And there, that one hanging in the middle there, is a drawing he did of me when I was in his *Phèdre.*" It is indeed: a lovely pastel, signed by Jean Cocteau. I am beginning to feel that I am in a museum—a museum which represents the work of a wide variety of prominent twentieth-century artists, but in which every artist has willfully and rather eccentrically chosen to focus on a single female figure.

It is a museum, however, from which the chief curator is absent. "Mama died four years ago," Toumanova tells me, in tones so freshly mournful that I feel compelled to express my condolences. "There has never been a personality like my mother," she continues. "It's not because she was my mother. It's because she was my friend."

It was her mother who tended not only the garden outside the house but the artifacts within. Toumanova has tried to take over these roles, but there is a sad frustration inherent in being the sole curator of one's own memories. "Some people say, 'I have done this, I have done that,' but they have no proof," she points out to me. "I have so much proof it is almost difficult for me." She sighs. "I am going through a difficult time right now. Everything I did, everything I created, everything I expressed is like a dream."

To cheer her up we turn to stories about her Hollywood career—from her role in Gene Kelly's *Invitation to the Dance* ("The second part is he and me, and he is at his best"), to the costume Mitchell Leisen commissioned for her in *Tonight We Sing* ("Exactly like Pavlova"), to the humor and brilliance of Billy Wilder, who directed her in her last film, the 1970 *Private Life of Sherlock Holmes.*

I ask her what it was like to work with Alfred Hitchcock in *Torn Curtain,* a 1966 thriller in which Toumanova plays an imperious Czechoslovakian dancer who delivers Paul Newman up to the enemy. The look Hitchcock drew from her in the film—a harsh, arrogant stare, repeatedly focused on Newman during a series of stop-motion pirouettes—is the exact opposite of the dreamy, sultry look captured by George Lynes in his photograph. How, I wondered, had the director prepared her for this role?

"He adored me," Toumanova says of Hitchcock, "because I was a part of the life he admired. I had the letters of Jean Cocteau, Miró, Chagall, Darius Milhaud. And he said to me, 'Madam, do you know what you have? You are a very rich young lady.' And I said, 'Yes, *Maître,* I know what I have.'" Toumanova also recalls that when she was on the set, surrounded by the crew and the other players,

Hitchcock would have his secretary bring out a silver tray bearing a single glass of champagne: "Only one glass. That means nobody else but me. That is how he thanked me."

When I bring up the photography of George Platt Lynes, Tamara Toumanova first assumes that I'm referring to another portrait he did of her, a 1941 photograph taken while she was in Salvador Dali's *Labyrinth.* She owns that photo ("The original," she says, as if a photograph could have only one) and has seen it reproduced many times. But then I produce the earlier picture that had hung in the Kopeikin show, and she is both startled and moved, for she has not seen this picture in decades. After studying the photo for a moment, she identifies it as being from *Cotillon,* the first ballet Balanchine made for her, in 1932. What is odd, she comments, is that in the photo she is wearing not her own costume (that of a young girl at her first ball), but the costume of another role, "the woman in black." Balanchine, apparently, was not present during the photography session; it was Lynes who got her to pose in this theatrical, purely invented position. Toumanova nonetheless agrees with Balanchine's assessment of Lynes's choreographic evocation. "It's so outstanding," she says, looking at the picture. "I don't say this because it is me, but because it is a beautiful picture. The hand, resting . . . the quality of the look. They don't take photographs like that anymore."

Later she elaborates on this theme. "It is an epoch that is going away. I look at it and it is like another world." She looks at me hard, as if to instill in me the importance of what she is about to say. "In life, you never realize how everything changes. It changes suddenly."

I look down at the photograph in my hand, at the dreamy look, the softly resting hand, the delicately balanced pose, and I realize that the woman in the photograph is silently telling me just the opposite. *I will be this way forever*, she is saying.

A NIGHT AT THE OPERA

I was not, as a child, taken to the opera. This was only partly a matter of money. It is true that we did not have enough to buy good seats, but there is always the balcony, or even standing room, for those who are passionate about the art form. My husband, for instance, comes from a working-class Italian-American family—a background much poorer, economically, than mine—and *he* was introduced to opera as a child. Toward the end of her life my mother-in-law, even when she was subsisting entirely on social security, would give opera tickets as gifts to relatives. (Ambiguously malicious gifts, sometimes, but that's another issue.) And several friends of mine from equally impecunious backgrounds recall that, as teenagers, they would sneak into performances during intermission, so that by the time they were in their twenties they knew the second halves of a number of operas. And then there were always records.

But we didn't even have opera recordings, which suggests to me that my lack of early exposure to the form was more, or other, than an issue of just money. I remember being told that my father couldn't stand the sound of the human voice accompanying classical music; he felt it marred the instrumental experience. (In this respect, at least, he is the opposite of Mark Morris.) And my father is the more overtly musical of my parents: he is—or was—a competent amateur on the recorder. After the divorce, when he was living alone in New York, he used to spend many of his Saturdays driving upstate to a monastery in order to play recorder duets with one of the monks; afterward he would share the brothers' wordless midday repast (it was an order that had taken a vow of silence, which no doubt added to my father's pleasure) and then drive back home to his solitary apartment.

My sister inherited this musical talent. She also developed, as a child, a passion for Gilbert and Sullivan operettas, and had collected nearly a full set of those old, rather lavishly boxed D'Oyly Carte LPs by the time she was thirteen. Among the several instruments she played was the cello, and she would use it to do a hilarious imitation of The Lady Jane in *Patience*—hilarious partly because my sister, though very thin, nonetheless managed to convey something of the role's plump bathos. Perhaps as a result of her interest, or perhaps as a cause of it, we *were* taken to see live touring productions of Gilbert and Sullivan. But not to the opera per se.

So it was not until I was well into my twenties, maybe even in my early thirties, that I first attended an opera at the venerable San Francisco Opera House. (Before that, there had been one evening at the Paris Opera when I was a Eurailing student of twenty—but I was so high up, and so ignorant of what I was seeing, that I remember more about the Chagall ceiling than I do about the opera being performed.) Now I try to go at least once or twice a year. Sometimes the operas are good and sometimes they are terrible, but I find that I like the experience of being at the opera.

I have particularly fond memories of an evening a few years ago when my husband and I went to hear *Tosca*. The source of my affection was not the opera; in fact, after a subsequent exposure to *Madame Butterfly* I have decided to swear off Puccini altogether. No, the warm feelings I associate with that occasion have to do with the opera house itself, and in particular with the people who have for many years carried on its underlying functions. My night at the opera, that night, was spent mainly outside the glamorous multi-tiered auditorium, in the belly of the building.

My own belly was the initial problem: from the moment I sat down, I began to experience a severe case of stomach cramps. At the first intermission I leapt out of my seat before the applause had decently ended so as to be among the first in the ladies' room downstairs. Then, to kill the rest of the interval and exercise my complaining stomach muscles (why *had* I insisted on having that West Indian curry for dinner at six o'clock?), I strolled around the basement bar, attempting to look as if I had a purpose. In my peregrinations I noticed a little room marked First Aid just to the left of the bar area, where people appeared to be getting medical attention, or at any rate attention. I longed to be there—to go in and lie down for a while. But I couldn't bring myself to overcome the shame of walking into the First Aid room amid all those well-dressed witnesses, particularly since I wasn't visibly having a heart attack or anything.

So I went back to my seat. But as the lights began to dim I said to my husband, "I think I'll go lie down in the First Aid room for the second act. My stomach is killing me." I had realized, you see, that during the performance all those people would be gone from the bar, and therefore no one would observe my shameful defection. I scurried up the aisle toward the exit doors just as Scarpia sounded his first notes.

The bar was, as I had hoped, deserted, and the door marked First Aid remained invitingly open. I peeked my head inside and was greeted by a chipper, owlish man in, I would guess, early middle age. He had round spectacles and a receding hairline, and seemed to be about my height—though it may only have been his extremely unthreatening air that made him seem comfortingly short.

"I have stomach cramps," I announced. "Do you think I could lie down here for the second act?"

"Of course!" He gestured toward two old-fashioned

slatted bedsteads (they reminded me of my visits to British infirmaries) that had been screened from my view when I stood in the doorway. "We have Herbert Hoover–vintage beds. Grey institutional blankets from 1932" (which, as the program had reminded me, was the year the San Francisco Opera House opened; *Tosca* was the first performance). "Everything for your finest comfort. What have you been eating?"

"Caribbean food," I answered, glad that he didn't immediately attribute my stomachache to either menstrual cramps or emotional instability.

He set a little footstool next to the nearer bed, the one most shielded by the screen. "Just take off your shoes and climb up," he said. "Do you want to get under the covers? Or would you like me to cover you with a blanket from the other bed?"

"A blanket from the other bed," I agreed happily. Lying down in my dress wasn't so bad. In fact, lying down and being covered by a blanket was wonderful. My stomach instantly ceased to bother me.

After enjoying my supine position for a moment or two, I turned my head to look at my protector. Seated at a little desk directly in line with the door but also within my view, he was writing in what looked like a large guest register.

"What's your name?" he asked.

"Wendy," I said conversationally.

"No, I mean your last name," with a smile.

"Oh—Lesser." He appeared to be writing it down; perhaps he was noting my symptoms in some kind of catalog.

"Do you get many people down here in the course of a performance?" I asked.

"Oh, yes, quite a few. Opera lovers are very passionate people, and unexpected things are always happening to passionate people. Opera lovers like to overdo everything—food, love, emotion . . ."

"Especially *Tosca* lovers," I hazarded.

"All opera lovers," he said. "Very passionate people. I admire that. I wish I felt equally passionate about something. But I don't—at least not at the moment."

I decided this was a good place for the conversation to end. Turning my head back toward the screen next to my bed, I closed my eyes. But even with them closed I could still sense the light in the room and the comforting presence at the desk.

When I was ten I stayed overnight in a hospital after an operation to remove my adenoids. ("Largest pair of adenoids I ever saw," the doctor remarked to my mother.) What I chiefly remember from the experience, and what I remember noticing most at the time, was the extraordinary comfort of lying asleep in a bed while outside my room, visible through the glass, a nurse stayed awake all night at a lighted desk. I was only ten years old, but I was already conscious of how pleasurable it was—and how rare a pleasure—to be watched over by impersonal, protective forces while I slept.

While I was recalling this I heard someone come to the door of the First Aid room. "Oh, are you alone?" she said in a normal conversational tone, and then, on spotting me, "Oh, sorry!" in a whisper.

"It's okay," he said. "You can come in."

I kept my eyes shut and breathed as if asleep. I couldn't quite distinguish her whispered words at first, but soon, in her agitation, she grew louder.

"I'm just so upset," she said. "No one even told me, and then I go to look on the chart for next week, and I'm only On Call. No regular shifts at all. And the rent is due, and I've had a lot of expenses this month, and I *really* need the money. And I hate to be On Call because you're supposed to be by the phone all day, but I go to class every morning, and in the afternoon I like to go to the library. Like today I was at the library until five-thirty, and then I got here at seven. But what really hurts me is that no one said my work is bad or anything, they just gave me that schedule. So I don't know why, or if I'm going to lose the job, or what."

"I can see you're very upset," he said. "Now, I don't really know how things work around here, because I'm not actually part of the staff. But I think that if you talked to someone you trusted—do you know Zooty?"

"Yes, I know Zooty. I can talk to her. She's always been straight with me. But she's not around tonight."

"Well, if you look on the schedule you can see when she'll be in—tomorrow or the next day—and then you can just go up to her and say, 'Zooty, I have to talk to you about this.' And that way you'll at least find out, one way or the other, what it means. I can see a large part of what's bothering you is the uncertainty."

"Yes, the uncertainty, and no one told me about it. I mean, if they had said, do you want this shift or that shift, I could be flexible, but just to read on the chart that I'm On Call . . . I don't want to lose my job here. I mean, it's not just the money. I like it much better than any other job I've ever had. Much better than McDonald's—a whole different atmosphere, with all the rich people acting polite. And much, *much* better than telemarketing. That was my last job. You never meet any of the other people working there, you're just in a little room by yourself with a telephone, you go in, you go out. Here it's such a nice, friendly group and we all talk together, and I don't want to leave."

"Well, would you be willing to do any kind of work here?" he asked. "Because if you say to Susan—do you know Susan? she runs the kitchen—if you say, 'Susan, I'm willing to work in the kitchen when you need people,' then that's another place they could put you, if they don't have a regular shift available. You should talk to Susan *and* Zooty. And when you talk to Zooty, here's my secret advice: Zooty cares a lot about education, so let her know you're going to school in the morning, and I think she'll respect that."

"Yes, I need for people to respect my goals. I need for people to respect *me*. That's what really hurts me about all this." There was a moment of what might have been silent sniffling.

"I certainly understand why you're feeling hurt," he said. "I can see that. You just need to get some clarity. So just resolve that you'll talk to them and that way, tomorrow or the next day, you'll at least be able to settle your mind, one way or the other. And then you'll know where you are, and what you have to do next."

"Yes," she said. I heard her chair scrape as she got up. "Thanks," she said. "It really helped to talk to you about it."

"My pleasure," he said.

Someone went by the door then. "The doctor is in," I heard a voice say, somewhat mockingly. Or maybe it was just a standard greeting. That voice passed quickly out of range, and the first confessor left the room. I cracked my eyelids and peered through my lashes at this surprising person, now alone again at his desk, apparently reading.

So this was where all the action was at the opera. Forget the rusty plot proceeding on stage; *this* was the locus of the soul-searing story, *this* the place where real emotions were bared and acted upon. I thought about my guardian angel's gentle manner and friendly advice. What a story, I thought—it's like *The Barber of Seville* (remembering that barbers, several centuries ago, were also doctors of a kind); he's like Figaro, fixing up everybody's life, dispensing advice and plans. How could I do this as a modern *Barber*, with the plot translated to a contemporary opera house? Let's see, we could have an older man in the audience—a regular opera patron, one of those rich, elderly guys, a judge, say—and his young ward, whom he was secretly planning to marry. No, people don't have wards these days. Let's make him the head partner in a big law firm, and she's a young associate. She's not interested in him—she only came to the opera for business reasons—but he's threatening to oppose her partnership if she doesn't give in and sleep with him. She has a terrible headache and comes down to the First Aid room, and ends up telling the owlish little guy all about her problems. And *he* figures out a way that she can trick the old guy and marry the public defender of her dreams . . .

No, it wouldn't work. I was missing the heavy-moral-code dimension. What, in modern-day San Francisco, could possibly substitute for the Church in eighteenth- and nineteenth-century Europe? Nobody would be interested these days in the power, or the corruption, of the

moralistic old regime. Religion was a dead issue. My plot
foundered.

"Hey, have you ever read the Bible?" said a new voice
from the doorway.

I kid you not. I have not made this up. This is the exact
order of events.

"No, that's not really my sort of thing," said my reli-
able friend. "I know a lot of people find it comforting, but
I just can't get around the unscientific basis. I can't believe in stuff like that."

"No, I don't mean as religion. I mean just as literature,
as something to read." The new voice was much louder
and more confident than her predecessor's had been. She
was striding into the room as she spoke. "Oops!" she said
when she caught a glimpse of me.

"That's all right," he said, evidently convinced by now
that I could sleep through anything.

I heard her heave herself into the chair. "I mean, there's
some incredible stuff in there. You should really read it."

"I'm afraid this is more my speed," he said.

"*Death Be Not Cautious.* A murder mystery, huh?"

"Yeah, I like them."

"But you should see what they have in the Bible. The
Book of Revelation, for instance. That's scarier than anything in Stephen King. I was reading it aloud to my
young cousins once, in Ireland—they didn't have anything else to read in the house—and they got really

scared. All sorts of monsters with weird faces and stuff. And Samson and Delilah! That's one of my favorites. Have you read that one?"

"No," he said politely. "It's the one about how a lot of hair makes you powerful, right?"

I myself might have been hesitant to push this line of conversation with a man who was prematurely balding, but she soldiered on. "Yeah, and then Delilah cuts all his hair off. But you don't really feel she's being unfair. It's really interesting."

There followed some desultory conversation about how well or badly they had done in high school English classes, and how they had taken years to discover what they liked reading on their own, due to the misconceptions instilled in them by boring teachers. I believe there was a reference to a Robert Frost poem; I know there was some slighting discussion of *Moby-Dick* and *The Scarlet Letter.* I was less interested in the content of the conversation than in its tone. My medical man had transformed himself—from the gentle, knowledgeable dispenser of advice to the friendly, untutored amateur, eager to learn from another. His therapeutic consulting room had become an impromptu literary seminar.

"Oh, the intermission's about to start. I've got to go. See you!"

"Yeah, see you later," he answered.

It was only a few minutes before I heard the familiar sound of my husband's footsteps. He paused by the doorway.

"I think my wife . . ."

"You must be Mr. Lesser," said my faithful attendant. They were speaking simultaneously, as in an Altman film.

My husband, who has a different last name, is used to confusion. He finished his sentence, ". . . came in here to lie down?"

I sat up in bed and smiled. My husband was amazed at my transformation: I had been in a foul humor since before the Caribbean restaurant.

"The patient is fine," said my medical friend, smiling as well. "Did you have a good rest?"

"Excellent," I said, climbing down and reclaiming my shoes. "Thank you for letting me use your nice bed."

"Vintage 1932," he told my husband. Then he turned to me: "And you, Mrs. Lesser, should watch what you eat for the next twenty-four hours or so. No coffee, if you can help it, and no spicy foods."

"Okay," I said cheerfully, not necessarily intending to comply. At the door I turned back and waved. He gave me a big grin and a thumbs-up sign.

"Quite a bedside manner he has," said my husband.

"You don't know the half of it," I said.

RALPH

It is commonly observed that people resemble their pets—that they acquire cats and dogs who look like them in the first place, and that animal and owner become ever more alike as the years pass. I have noticed the phenomenon, but I think the etiology is slightly different. It is not that we really *look* like our pets, but that we come to understand our own characters by observing theirs. This may not even be a matter of resemblance, since the qualities one admires in an animal may be precisely those one lacks rather than possesses. Still, I think it is true that, over the years, pet owners increasingly define themselves in relation to their animal companions. However blindly you may have chosen your cat or dog in the beginning, his presence forces you into a certain degree of self-awareness, or at the very least self-examination. Animals make a good mirror in this way because they provide such a smooth, unbroken surface, a kind of living *tabula rasa* on which we can project our narcissistic perceptions and imaginings. So we may come to resemble our pets—or think we do—without actually borrowing their physical appearance.

I had a cat without a nose.

This was the only extraordinary thing about Ralph. He was intended from the beginning to be a merely normal cat. I called him Ralph to signal that—to reflect his ordinariness, and to ensure it.

Before Ralph I owned a cat named Melanctha, named for Gertrude Stein's wandering black heroine. My Melanctha also wandered. She would take up residence for days or weeks with neighbors, and I too would have to wander in order to find her, knocking on the doors of strangers who lived one street over.

"Does she lie on your chest and lick your neck when you're going to sleep?" I would ask, to make sure this was the right black cat.

"Yes!" the children of the household would always say. So I would take her home, without looking back at them.

I think she did this licking thing because she was the runt of the litter, and never got enough of her mother. But what does it matter? Do we reject love because its intensity stems from early childhood deprivation?

When Melanctha wasn't wandering, she sat beautifully on my kitchen windowsill, a perfect Egyptian figurine. She sat very still and stared out the window at nothing I could see.

My friend Katharine and I spent many hours in this kitchen, sitting catty-corner from each other at the built-in table, talking about our hopeless boyfriends. At one point we were both seeing musicians in the same rock band—I the bass player, Katharine the lead guitar. These two were part of a series that included a chess-playing mathematician (mine), a left-wing construction worker (hers), and two aspiring filmmakers (one for each of us). Each of these men had to be discussed in detail, over time, with many repetitions of the same sorry tale. "I have no idea what goes through his mind," Katharine would say. Once she added, looking at the cat, "It's like trying to read the inside of Melanctha's mind." "Melanctha's mind" became our shorthand for the whole subject of the obscurity of men.

One day Melanctha wandered too far. Or perhaps I romanticize the safety of home.

She was missing for weeks, and none of the neighbors had seen her. I would fall asleep at night thinking about the sandpapery scratch of her tongue on my neck. I found her body decaying in the bushes outside my house. "She must have been hit by a car," said my downstairs neighbor, who had run outside in response to my cry. "At least she came home to die," he added.

This made me weep harder. The children who lived next door, happening to be at that moment in their front yard, were embarrassed. "I'm sorry," I told their mother. "I'm all right," I told the children. "It's okay for grown-ups to cry." I made my downstairs neighbor take Melanctha's body to the SPCA for me. While he did it, I scrubbed the grout between my bathroom tiles with an old toothbrush. This is the only time I have ever done such a thing. Ralph was explicitly Melanctha's replacement. Katharine was not reticent in her comparisons. "Well, he's certainly not the cat Melanctha was," she would say. "Look at those ridiculous white leggings. He looks like an amateur Shakespearean actor whose tights are falling down."

"Yes," I would admit. At first his shortcomings irked me—that he was not all black, that he lacked dignity, that he was male. (All my childhood cats had been female. In fact, in the household I shared with my mother, my sister, and a succession of various and often multiple pets, even the guinea pigs were always female. Males were considered a mere biological necessity, introduced for breeding purposes and then returned to the pet store, or wherever they had come from.)

I did not choose Ralph, as I had Melanctha. He was assigned to me randomly, the only remaining kitten in a litter owned by my sister's soon-to-be-ex-boyfriend, a sweet ne'er-do-well who disappeared from our lives, leaving my cat as his only trace. At first this seemed yet another example of Ralph's inadequacy, his failure to replace Melanctha fully. But eventually I began to feel that the randomness, the ordinariness, was the whole point.

I, who was not (to say the least) good at dealing with the unplanned, had unexpectedly been given an easy example of it. Ralph was my chance to learn to lend myself to circumstances. His name, which had begun as a kind of insult, became a term of endearment.

A decade later Ralph was still essentially the same personality: affectionate to friends and strangers alike, happy with his small portion, unassuming. By this time I had married a man who was, among other things, allergic to cat hair. After a long period of resistance, I agreed to convert Ralph into an outdoor cat. Ralph was, as always, accommodating.

Friends who were slaves to their pets deplored but also admired my harsh decree. "We'd like to get our cats outside, too," they said. "We're trying to Ralphicize them." His solid name supported an exotic yet useful verb, halfway between "rusticate" and "ostracize."

My husband, who had been married before, already had a son when I married him—a boy of five when we first met. Once, shortly after his father and I had started seeing each other, they came to my house for dinner. "Make hamburgers or hot dogs," said the father, my not-yet-husband. "He won't eat anything else."

"Nonsense," I said. I cooked cheese soufflé. The boy wouldn't eat. Very politely, he touched nothing.

Instead, he watched Ralph eating. We were all clustered in that same little kitchen where Melanctha had once adorned the windowsill. Ralph attacked his kibble ravenously and incompetently, spilling it in a mad circle around his dish.

"Soon you'll meet my sister," I told the boy conversationally. "She's coming up here for a visit."

"Is she a messy eater too?" he asked.

"Too?"

"Like Ralph. I wondered if everyone in your family is like Ralph."

My stepson is now twenty-four, an adult with his own apartment, girlfriend, cat. I have my own son now. It is on him that Ralph's noselessness had its effect.

It began with a bleeding sore in 1990, the year my son turned five. I waited for the sore to heal, as even the most severe cat scratches eventually do. But this didn't. As one always does in such cases, I correctly suspected the worst.

My regular vet, Dr. Berger, a charming man who spends half the year trekking with wolves, was away. His replacement was a young fellow with excellent diagnostic skills and no tact.

"We'll have to do a biopsy to be certain," he said, "but I'm almost sure this is an extremely aggressive form of skin cancer. We see a lot of it here in California—the sun causes it. If you leave it alone he'll be dead in two months. It eats 'em up."

"What are my options?" I said, affecting rationality.

"Well, radiation is our top-of-the-line recommendation, but it's hard on the animal, and it costs a lot."

"How much?"

"Oh—this is only ballpark, you know, I couldn't make any firm estimates—but somewhere in the $1500 to $1800 range."

"And that's my only choice? Radiation or he dies?"

"Well, Dr. Berger has a friend in Arizona who's done some experimental surgery on cats with this kind of cancer. He cuts off their noses. Seems to work in just about all the cases so far."

"How much does that cost?" I asked.

"Oh, say half as much—$700 or $800."

I didn't really have seven hundred dollars, let alone fifteen hundred dollars—not to spend on "a cat," especially "an old cat." But when I stopped obsessing about the money I realized I didn't have a choice: I couldn't just let him die. And I also realized that the money was a safe distraction, a screen for all the other things I was trying to keep myself from obsessing about.

"If we cut off his nose, he doesn't have to have radiation too?" I asked the young whippersnapper.

"Nope. See, in a cat this age, he's going to die of old age anyway before the cancer has a chance to recur. Now, if it were a child—"

"All right," I shut him off. "Let me talk to Dr. Berger about it."

Back from his wolves, Dr. Berger assured me Ralph would be cute without a nose. That was the word he used: "cute." I cleared out my savings account. The operation was a success.

Cute is not the word that would have jumped to my mind when I first saw Ralph after the surgery. Horrifying, maybe. Repellent. Abnormal. There was a bleeding hole in the middle of his face. As I was leaving to take him home, other patrons in the vet's waiting room turned away in disgust or fear.

When I first came to Berkeley, over twenty years ago, I would sometimes run into a man on the street who had no face. He lived in one of the downtown hotels near the campus, and he could often be seen shuffling up and down Telegraph Avenue. Everyone who lived in Berkeley at that time remembers this man. I was told then—I never learned if it was true—that he was a former chemistry professor who had been in a terrible accident. I pitied this man, or thought I pitied the person I imagined him to be, and I tried not to look away when I passed him on the street. But I couldn't help it. My eyes flickered involuntarily. Once I wrote down, in a notebook I was keeping at the time, a metaphor: "His eyes, surprising in the corrugated face—like a car whose headlights still gleam out from the midst of a badly crumpled fender."

When Ralph came home from his operation, I took him to my office to live. (I say "office," but it was in fact my apartment, left over from pre-marriage days, strenuously held on to as a remnant of my independent life.) I had two reasons for taking him there. One was that I wanted to keep him indoors and I couldn't do that with an allergic husband at home. The other was that I didn't want my son to see him right away.

"You can see him when he's healed," I said.

"Will he ever get his nose back?" my son asked.

"No," I said. "But he'll look better when it heals." And he did.

But still not cute. "He looks kind of terrible," my son remarked when he first saw him. "Do you think he minds?"

"I don't think so," I said. "I don't think he knows." But just in case, I tried not to mention the word "nose" in front of Ralph.

Other people were not so delicate. "What's *wrong* with that *cat?*" said someone who had come by to make a delivery. "He looks like something out of the movie *Dick Tracy.*"

A few months later my sister and her husband came to visit from Los Angeles, bringing along their four-year-old daughter. "Do you want to come over to the office with me to feed Ralph?" I asked the children. My son told his younger cousin all about the operation. She agreed to come, but preferred not to see Ralph. (My niece is, like her mother, a very sympathetic and gentle soul.) While

THE AMATEUR

my son and I called him, she turned away her face. But
by mistake she caught a glimpse. Then she reached down
to pet him. "I was afraid at first, but really he's kind of
cute," she said afterward.

Toward the end of that school year, on my son's
kindergarten classroom wall, appeared a poster the
teacher had made for the children. In one column were
things that made them happy, accompanied by a smiling
face. In the other were things that made them sad, with
a frown. "When somebody you love dies" and "When a
pet dies" were two of the entries in the sad column. At
the end of the happy column, my son had contributed:
"When a pet gets well."

For me, Ralph never got completely well. I missed the
nose. I missed the way he used to look—any cat has it,
that beautiful Egyptian profile. When Ralph sat on my
chest and purred, I didn't like looking up into those two
rosy, gaping nostrils. And I hated the way he sounded
when he sneezed. But I learned to live with it remarkably
well, for me. Accommodation was never my strong point;
it was always Ralph's. But by the time he died—of old
age, as the vet had promised—we had long since met
halfway.

THE CONVERSION

This is not to say that I am entirely reformed. I am still one of the stubbornest people I know. My first response to any suggestion or criticism or recommendation is generally to say no; only later does it occur to me that it might have been a good idea. Change is always difficult for me, and resistance is at the core of my personality.

I resisted e-mail for at least two or three years. Many of my Berkeley friends are academics, so they got it automatically as part of their jobs and then annoyingly sang its praises. "It replaces long-distance phone calls!" "You can dig up old recipes from libraries across the Midwest!" "It allows you to communicate instantaneously with colleagues from South Africa!" None of these seemed like things I particularly wanted to do. Moreover, I had strong if somewhat irrational reasons for resisting. I did not want my computer talking on the phone to anyone else's computer, because who knew what could happen once you opened up those lines? I wasn't just worried about viruses, though those were indeed a concern; but how could you be sure that someone wouldn't sneak through the e-mail door and thereby penetrate your hard disk, stealing or at any rate messing up your closely held documents? I preferred to keep my computer chaste and self-contained, aloof from all potential communicants.

And then, I didn't see the point of getting those unreadable little messages that seemed to go on forever, with little or no punctuation. To judge by the e-mail I had read in newspapers and magazines (the kind that was always reproduced to show how fun and liberating this new mode of communication was), these emissions were somewhere below the level of the worst unsolicited manuscripts I receive in the course of editing a literary magazine. Why should I want to read more of the stuff, especially on a barely legible computer screen? What was the good of a technological form that erased the boundary between intimate friends and total strangers, reducing everyone to a digital printout? Where was *handwriting* in all this? Where was *personal style*?

I should interrupt my screed to say that I am not a complete antitechnologist. I watch more television than just about anyone I know, and believe that *Hill Street Blues* and *NYPD Blue* are among the substantial artistic achievements of late-twentieth-century America. I use the latest (well, the second-latest) desktop publishing equipment to put out my magazine, and rely on a rather complex database software to organize its subscriber list. I adore the fax machine and have long considered it the single greatest invention since the telephone—the fax machine, after all, respects and transmits handwriting, just as the telephone conveys the nuances of the individual voice. I am not, that is, a hermit. I constantly employ and enjoy electronic transmissions of many sorts, and I do not feel that they in any way sap my capacity to be an Emersonian individual. On the contrary, they enhance it: without all my little machines, I could not make a living as a self-employed, self-designated arbiter of cultural taste. In Emerson's time you had to inherit a comfortable income if you wished to subsist as a man of letters; in our day technology can substitute for and even generate the freeing effects of wealth.

But for some reason this dashing perspective, this resolutely cheerful optimism about mechanical progress, did not make a dent in my fear of e-mail. From the viewpoint of one who has now crossed the great divide, I can see that my phobia stemmed in part from a category error. That is, I thought that "e-mail" and "the Internet" were identical: I believed that in order to communicate with my friends and colleagues I would have to place myself squarely in front of all the oncoming lanes of traffic in the Information Superhighway. Worse: I was persuaded that those snippets of generic e-mail clipped from the bulletin boards of the Internet represented what my own friends would sound like if I had to talk to them by computer. I wrongly supposed that the machine controlled its own content, that the medium (as we used to say, *pace* McLuhan, in the Sixties) would be the message. Why I should have believed Marshall McLuhan in this respect when I had long since discarded his views on television is a question that perhaps requires a cultural psychotherapist to answer. (I don't know that there *is* such a thing as a cultural psychotherapist, but since I have recently learned of something called "ecopsychology"— which is designed to help us bond with Mother Earth—I assume there are no limits.) For some reason, fear makes us believe in false prophets, the more apocalyptic the better. Clinging to the printed pages of my old-fashioned literary quarterly and my beloved cloth- and paperbound books, I thought that e-mail spelled the end of reading as I knew it. After all, you couldn't do it in the bathtub.

I still wouldn't want to read a novel or even a ten-page story on e-mail, and faced with that little message screen, I probably couldn't compose an essay worth printing. But for daily correspondence, electronic mail has become my essential instrument. Like all tools, it is more than just a simple replacement of the previous technology—it acts on you as well as you on it, and it acts in ways you can't always predict. In effect, e-mail has restored the personal letter to my life.

If you are like me, you went through a phase when

personal letters occupied a central place in your existence. You were probably in your late teens or early twenties. Possibly you were living away from home for the first time, or perhaps you had just embarked on your first long-term (and long-distance) love affair, or maybe you were traveling alone through Europe, or all of the above. The mail became your lifeline, and you honored it accordingly. You poured everything into your letters—the engaging details of daily existence, the special sights, the serious emotions, the witty observations—to such an extent that even journal-keeping, by comparison, seemed onerous and redundant. You tailored each letter to the personality of the recipient, delightedly imagining the eventual response to the in-jokes of a shared history. You received as good as you gave, and each day's mail delivery marked an emotional high or low point. And then, at some stage, you grew out of all this, and household bills, business letters, magazines, and fundraising pleas came to fill your mailbox.

Just as personal letters define a phase in an individual's life, so do they also define a period in Western history. I didn't realize this until I read P. N. Furbank's review of the *Oxford Book of Letters*, wherein he remarks "how deprived the ancient world was, not having discovered the secret of personal letters—long, spontaneous, chatty letters, as funny as they can be made but not always just funny, and coming nice and often—the sort of letters you

might have got if you had known Henry James or
Bernard Shaw or Philip Larkin. You would have been expected to answer them, and that would have been marvelous too, at least for oneself. It would be like enjoying
a second life." Exactly. And, as Furbank goes on to say,
"The ancients knew nothing of this. With what leaden
spirits one would have received a letter from Cicero! One
may hazard that this best kind of letter-writing began
in the eighteenth century and really came into its own
in the nineteenth." Not coincidentally, this was just
when the postal system was reaching a pinnacle of service, in terms of frequency and reliability.

For one of the keys to the pleasure of letters lies in that
half-buried little phrase, "and coming nice and often." In
London, where P. N. Furbank lives, mail is still delivered
twice a day, and a letter posted first class will reach its
destination anywhere in the United Kingdom by the next
day. It is still possible to keep up a satisfying personal correspondence under such circumstances. For the rest of
the world, however, mail is generally too slow to gratify
the needs of the moment. You might choose to rely on
the stamp and envelope on special occasions, or for particularly delicate communications, or if (like a young person in her teens or twenties) you live on a very limited
budget; but when you have something important to say,
you're much more likely to pick up the telephone.

The crisis in my attitude toward e-mail occurred when

I realized that I would no longer be able to afford the telephone. I was about to leave America for four months, and to indulge in long-distance calling from England would be ruinously expensive. Nor could I tolerate waiting the two weeks it would take for the round-trip communication by post. It was e-mail or nothing.

One problem with e-mail, though, is that it takes two actively willing participants. Anyone in the modern world can receive a postal letter, but only those with an e-mail hookup can receive e-mail. So I had to get my near and dear to join up at the same time I did. Among those I had to persuade was a writer in New York, a friend of over twenty years' standing on whom I normally lavish at least one long-distance phone call a day.

It always stops the conversation dead when I tell people, as I occasionally do, that I talk to Arthur every day on the phone. If my husband is present, he may get looks that imply, "What's the story here?" Or sometimes *I* get looks that say, "Aren't you a little old to have a 'best friend?'" But the truth is, I'm not: I need to have someone there at the other end of the phone line who can sympathetically but analytically respond to all the little exuberances and travails of my daily life. And so, apparently, does Arthur—either that or he's just humoring me. It's not easy to explain our connection. Some people might say that the pleasure lies in vicariously experiencing an alternate life (the straight California woman who writes for marginal literary publications versus the gay

New York man who works in the world of glossy commercial journalism), but that feels too schematic. I would say that, despite the obvious differences in our personalities (I am over-eager and intense, whereas Arthur routinely, and correctly, describes himself as "phlegmatic"), we share an essential element in our character; but that is no explanation, simply a circularly-arrived-at conclusion. Perhaps it's just that we know each other very intimately—as well we should, after decades of daily phone calls.

Since Arthur is even more of a technophobe than I am, persuading him to adopt e-mail was no easy task.

"I feel very resistant to the idea," he explained.

"I know, I know," I said. "I've already been resistant for three years, so can't we take it as done?"

Finally, I just cheated. I ordered *his* CompuServe introductory package when I ordered my own, knowing that when the user-friendly software slipped through his mail slot, he would be unable to resist trying it on. (Or, to put it more truthfully: I planned to make life miserable for him via telephone until he got around to applying his e-mail diskettes.)

It was slow to catch on. At first Arthur and I used e-mail mainly as a toy, in between the more substantial communication of our transcontinental phone calls, and most of our electronic conversation was metaconversation, in that it dealt with the ins and outs of using e-mail. But when I left California on a Wednesday night, arrived in London on the Thursday morning, hooked up my computer, received Arthur's welcoming message, and instantly e-mailed back—well, that was a revelation for both of us. Soon we were up to three or even four exchanges a day. The five-hour time difference meant nothing: he could post a note before he went to sleep, and I would receive it when I woke up the next day. And what I discovered, to my enormous pleasure, was that the electronic mode did not wash out his characteristic tones. On the contrary, he sounded in his virtual incarnation exactly as he did in real life: wry, observant, dryly affectionate, subtle, and sharp. Personal style, it turned out, did not get blotted out by the machine. In some ways it was even enhanced, with new opportunities for humorous self-expression and literary allusion afforded by the title spaces in our messages. "Internettled," his title bar announced when he had been fiddling all day to make the machine do something new. "Later the Same Day," I called one of my frequent messages, echoing Grace Paley. And it was inevitable, given the technology, that we would soon feel inspired to use E. M. Forster's "Only connect."

Even in our differing responses to the availability of e-mail, Arthur and I were faithful to our respective personalities. Something of a self-styled loner, he built up a tiny, highly selective list of e-mail addresses and mailed only to those two or three people. (His willful resistance to technological self-education may have had something to do with this. "How do you communicate with those outside our parish?" he once complained, stumped by the difficulty of crossing over from CompuServe to America Online or Prodigy.)

I, on the other hand, verged on epistolary promiscuity. Within my first week online in California, I had mailed to a number of my Berkeley pals, a long-lost classmate in Tasmania, three Londoners, my husband at his work address, my stepson at college, my father, my sister, a good friend who had temporarily moved to St. Louis, and my exercise teacher. I became an e-mail maniac, checking in every hour or so and collapsing with disappointment if I got the empty-mailbox beep. I found myself waxing expansive onscreen, chatting on about virtually nothing. I was responding, I now think, to the special enticements of the form's mixed nature—at once private and public, solitary and communal, so that it seems to combine the two oldest types of American writing, the diary and the sermon. With e-mail, you begin with the former, alone at your desk, and end (if you use your "multiple send" button) with the latter, broadcasting to the whole congregation.

One of the first responses I got from old e-mail hands, when I contacted them with my newly acquired address, was scorn at the impersonal nature of my mailing moniker. All of my friends, it appeared, had managed to craft idiosyncratic, sometimes poetic, always memorable labels for themselves. Using the loose conventions set up by most e-mail providers, they had come up with word combinations that were nearly as distinctive as their own names (and that often incorporated those names into the address). But CompuServe allowed for no such creativity: we were simply allocated a number. "Your address sounds like something from the Planet Zog," one of my correspondents wrote. Another mocked me for my long resistance to e-mail. "This is just the kind of address I would expect a confirmed Luddite to get," he noted. "Those who resist the machine are doomed to be punished by it."

Whatever form it takes, your e-mail address becomes a part of your permanent identity in a way that no mere phone number can. For one thing, you can't hide it. You can make an obscene phone call from an anonymous number or mail a poison pen letter without giving a return address, but your e-mail message carries its provenance in its heading. This necessary mutuality is both e-mail's virtue and its curse. That is, you have to consider before engaging in any communication whether you want to hear from someone as well as speak to him, because he will thereafter possess your address. There are no one-way assaults in the world of e-mail: if you launch a missive, you automatically open yourself up to a counterattack.

And unlike a phone number, which can be as temporary as your present whereabouts, your e-mail address travels with you. I had exactly the same CompuServe number during my London stay as during my normal Berkeley life. People seeking to contact me didn't have to know I was out of the country or even out of the office. Sometimes I would amuse myself by trying to imagine where my virtual mailbox was located. Did it float somewhere in the fourth dimension, rushing into my computer only when it was actually consulted? Or did it hover somewhere over the Atlantic, relaying messages between my temporarily European self and my North American correspondents ? I had been told it was in cyberspace—but what kind of space *was* that, exactly? Thinking such thoughts is a bit like trying to imagine how one's voice gets through those little telephone wires into the other person's receiver, only more so. You regress to your childhood self, for whom all such concepts are made concrete and miniature: the little person inside the telephone receiver, the tiny mailbox inside the computer. And the fact that my computer was a laptop (a ridiculously compact mechanism which, the dealer told me, was more powerful than the huge computer that had flown the first man to the moon) made the miniaturization imagery even more credible.

I discovered just how portable my e-mail was when a thief crept into my London house and walked off with my computer. One day I had been happily communicating with the entire world, the next I was reduced to virtual silence. My anxiety at the loss of my equipment was exacerbated by my sense of all the messages I was missing. I had become dependent on my daily fix, and the burglar, as if guessing at this aspect of my psychology, had even cut the phone wire that led into the computer—a symbolic act, easily remedied by the purchase of a new wire, but one that drove home for me my feeling of violent interruption. "I feel as if I'm hemorrhaging information," I told my husband. But information was only the half of it. All the little pieces of *me* that I had been feeding into cyberspace were loosed into the world, never to return.

Yet when I got a new computer, hooked myself back up to CompuServe, and checked my old mailbox, there it still was, just as if no interruption had ever occurred. My e-mail had been patiently waiting for me out there in Nowhere Land, the messages accumulating until I was once again able to pick them up. The beauty of the system, it turns out, is precisely that it's *not* connected to any physical object. They can steal the transmitting device from you, but the mail service continues unabated in its ideal Platonic form—temporarily inaccessible, maybe, but always ready to be picked up. I had my answer to Bishop Berkeley's question: if the tree had fallen in cyberspace, the sound could simply have waited decades or generations or millennia until someone came along to hear it, and *then* it would have existed. In this respect, as in so much else, e-mail's qualities are strangely mixed. It is both speedy to the point of instantaneousness and arrested in a state of timelessness.

So have I lost my soul to e-mail? I think not. Of course, proper use of it requires some mastery, and particularly self-mastery. One's initial subservience to the medium's surprising delights is inevitably a bit enslaving. (But this must have been true of all new media, even the cave paint at Lascaux.) Still, once it has been brought under control and made to function in the life you have already constructed for yourself, e-mail can be a great gift. If you keep all those strangers and business connections and mass-directory people off your screen, it can be, as Furbank put it, "like enjoying a second life." You will be rewarded with all the old-fashioned pleasures of the intimate personal letter. You will be offered, in other words, the chance to *gain* a soul rather than lose one. As an atheist, I'm not sure I believe in the very idea of a soul; but if I had to say where it resides, I would point to the thing in us that allows us to be and have intimate friends. And e-mail, by bringing back personal correspondence, reintroduces us to the form of writing that best enables us to know and acknowledge friendship.

CHASING DALDRY

Y ou may have wondered what I was doing in London for those four months. At times I even wondered myself; and I know my husband and son wondered why they had been forced to give up their comfortable Berkeley lives and relocate, however temporarily, to this antiquated, grimy, senselessly managed metropolis, with its beautiful old parks, horrible new buildings, interminable suburbs, overcrowded center, decaying transit system, strange domestic deficiencies, and stunningly rich cultural offerings. If I had a single answer, it was that we were there because of the theater.

It all started in 1993, when I went to London for a week on my own (my husband, in exchange, got a solo week in Sicily) and saw a production of *An Inspector Calls* at the National Theatre. I am used to relying on my own judgments, but rarely have I allowed a single judgment to determine so many of my future actions. I was both dazzled and moved by that production—it reminded me just how good theater can be, at its best—and within a few months I had decided that my next book would be about its director, Stephen Daldry.

My previous book had been about execution and murder (about execution *as* murder, really), so I was looking for a topic I could passionately love instead of passionately hate. I also had a vague idea that I wanted to write something about the performing arts, so that the written, permanent artifact I produced would complement the ephemeral art form it described rather than simply duplicating it, as my books about literature and painting had done. What I actually wanted to do, as I realized even then, was to write a book about Mark Morris. But that had already been done, quite beautifully, by Joan Acocella, so I was obliged to search out another brilliant young artist for myself. At the time I had no doubts about settling on a subject after only a brief exposure to his work. After all, I had fallen in love with Mark Morris's work on the basis of a single evening's encounter with *L'Allegro, il Penseroso, ed il Moderato*, and over the years that initial judgment had proven to be absolutely correct. Ergo, the same thing could happen with Daldry.

Logic is not always the best guide in these cases. Still, all the signs were good at the beginning. I sent Stephen Daldry a letter at the Royal Court—the venerable London theater of which, at the age of thirty-three, he was about to take command—asking if I could follow him around for a bit, with an eye toward writing an article or even a book. For the first and last time in our acquaintance, he responded immediately, with a note saying fine, when shall we start? I ascertained that he was about to go to New York to open *Inspector* on Broadway, and instantly scheduled a trip to coincide with that production's final rehearsals and earliest previews. (I was guided in this scheduling decision by my friend Arthur, who, having already profiled a couple of theater people for *The New Yorker*, could intelligently advise me on which rehearsals were crucial to see.)

One of my Berkeley friends refers to this trip as "the time Wendy went to New York and joined the circus." It's true that I came back bitten by the theatrical bug in a way that is hardly appropriate for someone my age. My week at the Royale Theater filled me with a new kind of energy and enthusiasm, with the sense that live drama was much more exciting than boring old printed literature. The frantic last-minute changes, the technologically complicated sets, the intense rehearsal periods, the worn old theater in its daytime incarnation, the feeling of an overall group ethic among the cast and crew, mingled with subsidiary alliances and spats: I loved it all. Anyone who got involved in theater as an adolescent will know what I am talking about. My son feels this way now about his drama classes and school plays. But my son is thirteen and I, at the time I am writing about, was already forty-two.

Stephen Daldry couldn't have been nicer on our first meeting. He took time off after a harried Saturday-night preview to have dinner with me at the restaurant across the street from the theater. He described the genesis of the *Inspector Calls* production. He told me his dreams. We discussed left-wing politics. He was charming, and I was charmed. We arranged that I would come over to London to see whatever he did next at the Royal Court.

That later trip—in November of 1994—gave me my first inkling of the problems I was to face. At the Royal Court, Daldry was no longer the free agent he had been in New York. He was hemmed in by all the responsibilities and personalities of an overworked, underfinanced institution, and he exacerbated the situation by making all decisions at the last possible moment. Rehearsals and even performances would be rescheduled at his command, and the mere act of making a short appointment to see him became a major undertaking.

"I don't know who's going to go crazy first, you or Stephen," said one of his kindly female assistants, commenting on the difficulties of my project, which had by now grown into a multi-year book.

"He is," I said grimly, "because I can always get out of here and go back to California."

Still, in for a penny, in for a pound. Besides, with my

usual eye for the philanthropic main chance, I had succeeded in getting a travel grant from a fellowship-giving
body. So I hauled my family off to London for the summer and early fall of 1995. The three of us saw a lot of
theater (I'd say we went to an average of three productions a week for the whole of that four months), and on
some days I even saw a little of Stephen Daldry.

The best times were when he was rehearsing a play. At
those moments, Daldry the adminstrator—the charming, prevaricating manipulator, the public relations expert, the phenomenal fundraiser—would drop away, and
Daldry the director would once again appear. Rehearsals
are essentially repetitions with changes, and it would be
easy to find them boring; on some days they *are* boring.
But as I watched a production emerge bit by bit, with
chance elements producing entirely new approaches and
large chunks of dialogue suddenly cut or rewritten, I
could feel the thrill of creation actually taking place. Art
came to life before my very eyes.

It will be objected that I, as a total outsider to the
theater, must have been a pretty poor observer. To this I
have two answers. One is that theater is finally *meant* for
the outsiders, for the audience members who attend only
once and who make their judgments instantaneously. In
those terms, anyone who has been an audience member
can potentially become a critic—and by this time I had
been an audience member at a lot of plays, starting when

I was a small child. The other argument is that the outsider brings something to the situation that the expert does not, so that she may be capable of seeing in fresher ways, and conveying what she sees in clearer terms, than the professional can. My model in this regard is and always has been George Orwell. In *The Road to Wigan Pier* (perhaps my favorite of his books), he tells us exactly what it feels like for a non-miner to go down into a mine, and it is the amateurish fear and wonder and disgust that make his account compelling.

I aspired to Orwellian description, but I never quite achieved it, perhaps because I lack the cool transparency that characterizes Orwell's prose. I am just not cut out to be a fly on the wall. I would sit quietly through six rehearsals, and then at the seventh I would burst out, "But what if you had him facing that way instead?" or "Oh, *no*! I can't believe you're going to cut *that* line!" Sometimes Daldry would give me a look that shut me up; other times he would take my advice. Once, I remember, he took four lines of notes I had given him and began copying them into his own handwriting—"So the actors will think they're *my* suggestions," he whispered conspiratorially. (Generally the scene turned out no better when he took my advice than when he ignored it, and he would usually have to put it back the way it was before.) For the most part Daldry more than tolerated me; he occasionally used me as a theatrical prop, allowed me to feed cough drops to the hoarse actors, and otherwise incorporated me into the close-knit family of the rehearsal room. I doubt that many other artists could have worked with someone like me around. *I* certainly wouldn't have allowed such an intrusive observer on *my* terrain, and I remain exceedingly grateful to Stephen for his unusual openness.

Whether the book turned out as I would have wished is another matter. The biggest problem was that Stephen Daldry never again did a production as good as *An Inspector Calls*—not, at least, during the four years I was watching him. If I had gargantuan faith in my powers, I might attribute this to the journalistic equivalent of the Heisenberg Uncertainty Principle: the theory would be that I was altering the story just by chronicling it. Much more likely, however, it was due to the peculiar conjunction of Stephen Daldry's own career, the Royal Court's history, and the artistic climate in London at the time, all of which meant that Daldry spent far more time on the building as a whole than on any plays of his own. He pretty much dried up as a director during the time I was following him around.

"I've got to renew my resources," he said to me in the last conversation we had, after I had already finished the book and he was explaining why he had decided to leave the Royal Court. "Right now I'm emptied out. I've got to feed myself, give myself something to work from again."

I hope his recuperation works; I hope that, before too

long, he manages to do a new production that is even more remarkable than his brilliant *Inspector*. But this is not because I am generous or kindly disposed toward Stephen Daldry. My motives are entirely selfish. I want him to succeed because I don't like feeling that my artistic judgments are randomly accurate rather than permanently true.

THOM GUNN

I dedicated my book about Daldry to the poet Thom Gunn for several reasons (in addition to the usual ones, that is, of affection and felt connection). Though he has never been in the theater himself, Thom has had long, strong ties with the theatrical world: his best friend from university days, Tony White, was an actor (until he died, tragically young, in a freak football accident), and his lover of over forty years, Mike Kitay, was a theater director for a while in the 1950s and 1960s. Also, Thom Gunn and Stephen Daldry seemed to me to have certain superficial qualities in common: they were both English, both gay (in a self-consciously masculine, determinedly un-"sissy" way), both charming and attractive to people of all ages and sexes, both rather childlike in their enthusiasms. But beyond this, I wanted to hold Thom Gunn up as a kind of example to Stephen Daldry. By leading off the Daldry book with the poet's name, I wanted to suggest to the gifted, energetic, but easily distracted young director that if it is possible to fritter away one's talents, it is also possible to concentrate them in the way Thom Gunn has done, using each passing decade to make the work deeper and richer and more reflective.

Thom Gunn might serve as an example to just about anyone, for he is that rare thing in the literary-artistic world, a truly virtuous person—"a nice man," as he is fond of saying about other people we know. But this does not mean he is inoffensive, or squeamishly polite, or any of the other wishy-washy qualities conjured up by the adjective "nice." If his work has a strong edge to it, this is in part because he has always been intrigued by bad behavior.

One of the more spectacular examples of this in recent years is his poem sequence about the serial killer Jeffrey Dahmer. Dahmer's cannibalistic murders form the basis of a series of four poems Thom Gunn published, under the title "Troubadour," in the Fall 1993 issue of *The Threepenny Review*. The poems recount some of Dahmer's antics in rather gruesome detail, and as we were typesetting them, we had a little betting pool in our three-person office about the number of subscribers who would cancel after the poems appeared. In the end there were no outright cancellations, but the poems did produce their share of outcry, both then and later.

"I rather like upsetting people," Gunn admitted, when

talking to me about the Dahmer poems several months after their publication. "I've always had a childish desire to shock. But I didn't really think those poems would upset people as much as they did. They weren't conceived of as being about somebody crazy, but about someone who experiences the things we do, only in more extreme form. I think of them as love poems. I mean, if you want to possess somebody, what better way than to kill them?"

Was there a connection, I asked, between his winning a MacArthur Fellowship in 1993 and his publishing the Dahmer poems shortly after that? Perhaps, I suggested, he wanted to show that he was still allied with the "undesirables" (as he entitled a little book of his poems about street people, derelicts, and other marginal types). Perhaps he felt guilty about winning America's biggest literary prize.

"No," he said flatly. "I don't feel at *all* guilty about the MacArthur. I do feel guilty about having a house whenever I pass by street people. But doesn't everyone feel that way?"

There is something very appealing about Thom Gunn's assumption that everyone is exactly like he is. But then, there is something boyishly appealing about Thom Gunn in general. His friends often entertain each other with stories about his curious mixture of ingenuousness and sophistication. August Kleinzahler—a younger poet whom Gunn considers a close friend as well as a helpful poetic advisor—gave me one such example.

"I was giving a reading at UC Berkeley," Kleinzahler recalled, "you know, in the Maud Fife Room. And I was extremely nervous. Thom was walking me to the room, down those long, empty corridors, and I felt like James Cagney in *The Public Enemy*—I could hear the click of my heels on the floor. Then Thom turns to me, very earnestly and solicitously, and says, in his most dulcet Oxbridge tones, 'Do you think you'll be wanting to have a wee-wee?' "

Something of Thom's youthful manner is apparent even in his looks. Though he'll be seventy soon, he's still thin and energetic, bounding up and down two flights of stairs at a moment's notice to retrieve a forgotten jacket or fetch a spare copy of a poem. His face is strongly lined, and his hair is the salt-and-pepper combination of Richard Gere's in *Internal Affairs*, a movie he much admires. (Actually, Thom hastens to point out, it would be completely grey if he didn't color it. "I think it's okay to dye your hair if you *tell* people it's dyed, don't you?" he says, in a confiding tone, to everybody.) But along with the greying hair he sports a gold ring in his left ear, a dragonish tattoo snaking up his right arm, and a wardrobe that consists mainly of T-shirts and black jeans—not your typical senior-citizen getup. Even his laugh is sudden, open, and childishly joyful, as well as loud enough to triumph over the din at any public gathering spot in San Francisco, the city he has made his permanent home since 1960.

Thom Gunn has always had a big, loud laugh. Karl
Miller, a classmate of his at Cambridge University in the
early 1950s (later the founder of the *London Review of
Books*), wrote of those Cambridge days: "A great pleasure
of the place was to watch Thom Gunn, of the sounding,
crashing laugh and lumberjack shirts, become a poet."
The lumberjack shirts are rarely seen these days, and the
process of becoming a poet has been satisfyingly, defini-
tively accomplished, but the laugh remains as fresh and
raucous as ever.

The spotlight has been on Gunn from a relatively early
age. By the time he was twenty-five he had published his
first book, *Fighting Terms*, and had been welcomed into
the company of a new generation of British poets that included Philip Larkin, Donald Davie, and Britain's current poet laureate, Ted Hughes. (It is perhaps a sign of
Gunn's achievement that by now all his contemporaries
in this group are either famous or dead, if not both.) In
1989 a prominent critic putting together a book about
British poetry since 1960 kept noticing "how insistently
Thom Gunn shouldered to centre-stage." At least a few
of Gunn's poems made it into virtually every anthology
of contemporary British verse, and some were even included in the standard O-level and A-level tests that determined a student's passage from secondary school to
university.

If you know a well-educated Englishman of a certain

age (say, forty to sixty-five), he is likely to be able to recite from memory at least a few lines of Thom Gunn—
the likeliest being a passage from the famous "On the
Move," the lead poem in his second collection. The poem
describes an alluringly ominous group of Hell's Angel–
like bikers, and it starts:

> *On motorcycles, up the road, they come:*
> *Small, black, as flies hanging in heat, the Boys* . . .

As if to signal that he too was on the move, Gunn himself briefly rode a motorcycle (though not until after he'd
written this reputation-making poem). "I rode it to show
off," he now says, "and I had it less than three months. I
shouldn't be trusted on the road. That's why I don't drive
a car. I think my reflexes are funny."

One Englishman who has been a fan of Gunn's since
the 1950s is the neurologist and writer Oliver Sacks. "My
battered copy of *The Sense of Movement* goes back to—
let's see, 1958," he told me. "Jonathan Miller, who was a
friend of mine, said, 'You must read this.' " Dr. Sacks subsequently ventured to San Francisco for a couple of years
of medical training, choosing the location in part because
Thom Gunn was already there. "I met him in 1961," recalls Sacks, who now lives in New York, "and I saw a fair
amount of him during my brief San Francisco days,
which ended in 1962. But I've kept in touch with him

since. And whether as a grand poet or the best of friends, he's someone I very much love and admire."

But in contrast to the English, most literate Americans—even most American fans of poetry, a far smaller group—had barely heard of Gunn. Elizabeth Bishop, writing to Marianne Moore from San Francisco in 1968, felt obliged to explain who he was, even though by that time he had already published five books. "One poet I've met here, almost a neighbor, I like very much, Thom Gunn," she wrote. "His poetry is usually very good, I think; he's English but has lived here for a long time." Gunn's opinion of Bishop was equally enthusiastic. "She was jolly and hearty and liked a good joke," he remembers. "And she gave the only really good literary party I ever went to." (Thom's dislike of literary parties has always been notorious, but his hermit-like behavior has increased in recent years, so that it now requires Herculean efforts to tempt him over to my house for a six-person Sunday lunch, even with people he likes. This is not because he is a homebody—he will take a one-hour busride on a rainy night to attend a friend's reading at a bookstore—but because he has clearly lost patience with most kinds of conventional social gathering. If he ever had it, that is: conventionality has never been his strong suit.)

———

When I first met him, in 1977 or 1978, Thom Gunn was eking out a living as a part-time lecturer in UC

Berkeley's English department, having given up a ten-
ured position there because he couldn't stand being on
committees. He had no health insurance, no retirement
plan, not even a single credit card (until, in the 1980s, he
finally acquired one so as to be able to purchase airline
tickets over the phone). He lived frugally, almost never
buying new clothing or hardcover books. His only tangible asset, a house in the Haight-Ashbury district, had
been purchased in the mid-1960s with a $3,300 down
payment carved from his $10,000 Guggenheim grant;
he shared out the mortgage among several rent-paying
housemates.

This is not, however, a tale of penurious merit ultimately rewarded, of ascetic renunciation for the good of
"Art." This is the tale of choices consciously made on the
basis of immediate as well as lasting desires; of pleasures
experienced and enjoyed; of a life explored and inhabited
so as to render up its manifold possibilities. During all
those years, Thom Gunn was having a ball—particularly
in the late 1960s and early 1970s, San Francisco's hippie
heyday.

I am unusually resistant to the allure of that period,
having come of age in its midst, but Thom won't let me
relax into my comfortable prejudices. "I liked LSD because it broke down categories," he tells me. "But that was
what I liked so much about the Sixties anyway. By your
mid-thirties you can get a bit smug, and the Sixties—and
by this I mean the drugs, the concerts in the park, all of

it—turned over my assumptions, delayed my middle-aged smugness a little." He manages to say this without animadverting to *my* middle-aged smugness, so I don't really feel it as a rebuke; rather, a stated difference between us.

The poems that came out of Gunn's period of discovery and self-discovery—poems about LSD, communal orgies, gay bathhouses, rock-star deaths, fragmentary memories, nightmarish visions, and the Northern California landscape, both urban and rural—took up much of the space in his next three books, which were published between 1971 and 1982. And these books did not endear him to his English public. The prevailing sense (as wittily summarized by Glyn Maxwell, a younger British poet) was that here was "a man of decorous, skillful, metrical verse who had for his own reasons become absorbed into an alien culture that gave him alien subjects (like sex), alien backdrops (like sunshine) and, most vexing of all, made his strict forms melt on the page. No longer could he be Our Man Out There like, say, Auden in New York or James Fenton in the Far East, because he seemed to have become Their Man Out There."

To an extent, this was the point of the whole endeavor: to escape being English. The freedom Gunn gained in 1960s San Francisco was in part the freedom to stop being what he had been brought up to be and become something else, something far less easily defined. He says as much in the last few lines of "The Geysers":

torn from the self
       in which I breathed and trod

   I am
           I am raw meat
               I am a god

Or, if not a god, then at any rate a Californian; at the very
least an "Anglo-American," as he now calls himself, in
imitation of the other models of ethnic immigration—
Italian-American, Hispanic-American, Asian-American
—that can be found so profusely in California.

It's not true, however, that California made all of
Gunn's British strictness melt away. As a teacher at UC
Berkeley he makes his students memorize passages of
poems, learn the crucial publication dates, and recognize
prosodic forms; I know this because, although I've never
been one of his official students, I've audited a couple of
his poetry courses. Joan Acocella, the dance critic, told
me that he was much the same when she took his English 100 course as an undergraduate in 1965. "He was extremely rigorous," Joan remembered. "He made us write
a two-page paper every week—he was very strict about
the two-page limit—and he always expected from us
more sophistication than the other professors did. He
gave us idiosyncratic material—more difficult, less lov-
able than the usual—and then he gave us his reasons
for liking it, which were bound up with his moral per-

sonality: his reserve, his distance. I'll never forget what
he taught me."

The students also found Gunn himself idiosyncratic,
and that too may have appealed to them. "He was different from the other professors," Acocella said. "He wore
leather, he was a poet, he was gay, and we knew that he
took the bus back to San Francisco every day." (To this
day, Thom Gunn takes the bus back and forth one semester each year to teach at Berkeley. He hasn't allowed
any of his recent fellowships to interfere with his scrupu-
lous, devoted teaching; once, in fact, he nearly turned
down a three-year fellowship when it seemed he would
have to stop teaching to accept it.)

The rigor which characterized his teaching was also
there, if less obviously, in his California-influenced poetry. He may have ceased to be wholly British, but he
could still produce "decorous, skilled, metrical verse."
Though the three books of the Seventies and Eighties
contain a great deal of free-verse experimentation, they
also contain a substantially higher proportion of rhyme
and meter than most American poets were using at that
time. Even in the lines I've quoted from "The Geysers,"
you can hear both the rhyme (of "trod" and "god") and
the old-fashioned, Shakespearean, five-beat iambic pen-
tameter ("I *am* I *am* raw *meat* I *am* a *god*").

Explaining why he chose to use meter when writing
about his LSD experiences, Thom Gunn has written,

"The acid trip is unstructured, it opens you up to countless possibilities, you hanker after the infinite. The only way I could give myself any control over the presentation of these experiences, and so be true to them, was by trying to render the infinite through the finite, the unstructured through the structured."

But this particular use of structure did not appeal to those who had praised Gunn's energy and adventurousness when he applied similar metrical forms to subjects like soldiers, bikers, and figures from Greek myth. What really bugged the British critics was Gunn's unashamed focus on pleasure and enjoyment; "good news is no news," as one English reviewer wryly put it in the *TLS*. It was not until Thom Gunn's next book, *The Man with Night Sweats* (which came out in England in 1992, ten years after *The Passages of Joy*), that the British wanted to hear what he had to report.

"Now that HIV and AIDS have turned Gunn's home into a place where we do send correspondents, at least when we feel up to it," the same review continues, "there he still is, an exceptional and fascinating poet with a formal range to rival Auden's, a sensuality equal to Ginsberg's, and a profound yet daily humanity that surely surpasses that of any other poet of our time."

I read this praise aloud to the fiction writer Leonard Michaels, who had taught with Gunn at UC Berkeley for nearly three decades. Lenny and I have many literary tastes in common, and one is our zeal for the poetry of Thom Gunn. Hearing the *TLS*'s ringing endorsement of our position, he shrugged with disdainful pity for the previously unenlightened. "Haven't I been saying *exactly that* all along?" he said with his characteristic Lower East Side inflections. Another shrug, as if to say, Who could miss it?

Apparently nobody, at the moment. After he won the $369,000 MacArthur Fellowship in 1993, the word "genius," in large, boldfaced type, appeared next to Thom Gunn's picture in several California newspapers, while the *Observer* in London headlined its interview with him "A poet who's still firing on all cylinders" (either a reference to those everlasting bikers, or else the standard pun on his last name). And then, in 1994, the publication of his *Collected Poems* resulted in that rave review in the *TLS*, a public reading with Rita Dove at Grand Central Station in New York, respectful notices in Sunday book sections across the country, and—to Thom Gunn's great delight—a one-page profile in *Spin* magazine, featuring a photograph that Robert Mapplethorpe took of him in 1980.

Thom was particularly pleased by the attention from *Spin* because he himself has long been an aficionado of rock music and an avid watcher of MTV. "The people at *Spin* thought I was terribly old-fashioned because I read *Rolling Stone*," he tells me with sly self-deprecation, all too aware that I know vastly less about rock music than he does. By my standards, Thom Gunn is frighteningly up-to-date. When he's not rereading Victorian novels or discovering Darwin's *Voyage of the Beagle* (the best book he read in 1991, he announced), he's spotting the latest good television show. "*NYPD Blue*, of course, I adore," he said a few seasons ago. "It doesn't worry me that it's violent any more than that *King Lear* is violent. I love the way it preaches—it preaches so well." He also watched *Seinfeld* ("like everybody else"), but noted that *The Simpsons*, which he once admired, had "lost its edge." Recently I asked him about *Brooklyn South*, and was not surprised to hear that he and Mike Kitay were avid fans. They've liked all the cop shows Steven Bochco has done since *Hill Street Blues*, as have my husband and I. In fact, the four of us may be the only people in America who loved *Cop Rock*: we mourned its speedy demise by watching the last episode together over dinner.

Thom habitually ferrets out the best in every genre, from Philip K. Dick to Thomas Hardy, and eagerly recommends a movie like the Harvey Keitel sleaze-fest *Bad Lieutenant*, praising its "hilarious Dostoyevskian humor." I can't say I always agree with his taste. The other night, watching a rented video of *The Fifth Element* purely on the basis of his hearty recommendation, I said to myself, "*What* can he have been *thinking*?" But I do agree with the principles that guide his judgments. Thom takes

pride in his refusal to distinguish between a nineteenth-
century novel and a recent potboiler, between a pop song
and a classical composition. "I hate the distinction between high art and low art, and I have since I was in my
teens. Dickens had the audience of Judith Krantz in his
time—Trollope held him in rather low esteem because
he was too crude and too popular," he gleefully points
out.

Such attitudes by no means prevent Thom from having strong opinions about the quality of any given artwork. When he and I get together for lunch every couple
of months, much of the conversation centers on which
books (and movies, and TV shows) we have loved or
hated. We both read for pleasure; at the same time, we
both believe in applying words like "good" and "bad" as
if they have a larger evaluative meaning, beyond our own
immediate mood. Whether I think this way in part *because* Thom does, or whether we arrived independently
at our position, is by now too complicated for me to figure out.

———

Before he got the MacArthur I used to worry about how
Thom would survive his retirement. As a part-time lecturer, he worked for most of his academic career without
accruing any pension. When he did accumulate any savings, he would spend the money in some nonsensical way,

like paying cash for a city-mandated structural repair to his house when he could have taken out a no-interest loan. This kind of thing used to drive me crazy, but Thom was never anxious about his finances. "I always said, when people asked how I would support myself in my old age, that my public would take care of me. And now it has!" he laughed after getting the MacArthur. The unexpected windfall also paid for him and Mike to take a special trip to Venice, where they hadn't been since they were in their twenties, and Prague, which they saw for the first time in 1993. Recently they went back to Venice to celebrate the final year of the MacArthur fellowship. "Mike said it was like walking with his ninety-year-old mother," Thom reported to me. "He would walk very quickly, and I kept wanting to sit down every hour and have some more wine. But I think we covered just about every street in Venice."

Remarking on his good fortune to a British journalist who interviewed him after he won the first Forward Prize in 1992, Thom Gunn said, "I've travelled, I've been happily in love for forty years, *and* I've read *The Brothers Karamazov* three times." The joke at the end (which is only partly a joke: Thom takes his reading very seriously) undercuts the sentiment a bit, but it is true that he has been in love for more than forty years. He met Mike Kitay, an American studying at Cambridge, in 1952. Because Kitay had returned to America to do his military service,

Gunn came to Stanford for graduate work in 1954. The
two of them eventually settled in San Francisco, where
Mike had a job scriptwriting for television.

"It is not easy to speak of a relationship so long-
lasting, so deep, and so complex, nor of the changes it
has gone through, let alone of the effect it has had on my
writing," Thom Gunn has written about his life with
Mike Kitay. "But his was, from the start, the example of
the searching worrying improvising intelligence playing
upon the emotions which in turn reflect back on the intelligence. It was an example at times as rawly passionate as only Henry James can dare to be." (He's not kidding
about Henry James. Gunn rereads *The Wings of the Dove*
every few years, and *The Awkward Age* is one of his two
favorite novels of 1899; the other is Rudyard Kipling's
Kim.)

A number of Thom's poems are love poems to Mike,
including "Thoughts on Unpacking," "The Separation,"
"Touch," "The Hug," and a newer one called "In Trust."
I heard "In Trust" for the first time at a poetry reading
on the Berkeley campus and was extremely moved by
it—partly, I imagine, because I was sitting next to Mike
Kitay during the reading.

Mike, who still looks very much as he did when Thom
described him in "To a Friend in Time of Trouble" ("A
handsome grey-haired, grey-eyed man, tight-knit") had
been giving me hints about who or what was being re-

ferred to in each of the previous poems. When this poem began, he fell silent.

> *You go from me*
> *In June for months on end*
> *To study equanimity*
> *Among high trees alone:*
> *I go out with a new boyfriend*
> *And stay all summer in the city where*
> *Home mostly on my own*
> *I watch the sunflowers flare.*

But if the poem begins with separation, it ends with a powerful coming together:

> *As you began*
> *You'll end the year with me.*
> *We'll hug each other while we can,*
> *Work or stray while we must.*
> *Nothing is, or ever will be,*
> *Mine, I suppose. No one can hold a heart,*
> *But what we hold in trust*
> *We do hold, even apart.*

Thom Gunn and Mike Kitay's complicated history is reflected in their domestic arrangement, which includes other people who have entered their lives along the

way—Thom's family, or "household." And this communal group is in turn embedded within the larger community of San Francisco, which Gunn also considers his
home. Gunn's two "obsessions," as he self-consciously
calls them, are both connected to this feeling of living
within the larger civic society. "I don't like people getting
movies in their own homes, and I don't like people driving around in cars," he announces. "I think people
should take public transportation and be with other
people in movie theaters. Merely sitting near another
person on a bus or in a movie theater is good for the sense
of community." Like all Thom's pronouncements, this
one has been susceptible to modification. He has given in
to the culture of the VCR, and often watches videos at
home now. (That's how he disinterred *The Fifth Element*.)
But he does still ride the bus everywhere, except when
Mike is along to give him a ride.

Thom Gunn's permanent household—where, as he
says in one poem, "Each cooks one night, and each cooks
well"—consists, at this point, of himself, Mike Kitay,
Bob Bair, and Bill Schuessler. Another housemate, Jim
Lay, died of AIDS on Christmas Day, 1986. "Four of
my friends died in one month," Gunn said of the epi-
demic that stimulated him to write the central poems
in *The Man with Night Sweats*. He himself is HIV-
negative, a fortuitously exempted bystander to the mass
tragedy, as he suggests in the poem "Courtesies of the
Interregnum":

Excluded from the invitation list
To the largest gathering of the decade, missed
From membership as if the club were full.
It is not that I am not eligible . . .

In the notes at the back of the *Collected Poems*, Thom
Gunn lists the names of the dead friends referred to in
his poems about AIDS. "For the record—for *my* record
if for no one else's, because they were not famous
people—I wish to name them here." He has always had
strong feelings about names, about the specific, individual identity assigned to one person and no other. "Poor
girl, poor girl, what was your name?" he asks in the last
line of "The Victim," his poem about Sid Vicious's murder of his girlfriend, and in the notes he supplies the answer. The actual, historical record, the particulars of an
individual personality, matter to Gunn, and this is one
reason his memorial poems have such power.

The same passion for specificity also explains another,
very different aspect of Thom Gunn's character: his enormous congeniality as a gossip. He remembers every tid-
bit of information ever passed on to him, every remark
ever made to him, and by whom; and he can retrieve it at
exactly the pertinent moment in a conversation. "I'm the
soul of indiscretion," he confides, and then listens eagerly
to the next gossipy secret.

That is one side of Thom Gunn. The other side is just
the opposite: a man who deeply believes in the virtues of

impersonality. In an essay called "My Life up to Now" he comments on the fact that he is very consciously "a rather derivative poet," and then goes on to say that "it has not been of primary interest to develop a unique poetic personality, and I rejoice in Eliot's lovely remark that art is the escape from personality."

You can find the same idea in his poem "Expression," which complains about "the poetry of my juniors," in which "Mother doesn't understand, / And they hate Daddy, the noted alcoholic." Tired of this confessional mode (the mode of most contemporary American poetry, from Robert Lowell and Sylvia Plath onward), the poem's speaker goes to an art museum, where he seeks out a medieval Italian painting of the Virgin and Child. The poems ends:

> *The sight quenches, like water*
> *after too much birthday cake.*
> *Solidly there, mother and child*
> *stare outward, two pairs of matching eyes*
> *void of expression.*

———

On the *assemblage*-style wall of Thom Gunn's second-floor study, amid cut-out pictures of River Phoenix and Keanu Reeves, antique postcards of nude bodybuilders, and assorted posters, clippings, and visual paraphernalia, is a photograph that doesn't go with the rest. In it, a beautiful dark-haired woman holds a pretty blond baby, both of them staring outward at the camera. I have been in the study before, to pick up a lent book or admire the view out the back window, but I have never before noticed the photograph. Now, however, we are spending longer than usual here, because Thom is giving a tour of the house to Tony Kushner. (Kushner, in town to deliver a lecture following the great success of *Angels in America*, told me that the person he most wanted to meet was Thom Gunn, so I arranged a lunch. In Kushner's view, "He is certainly one of the greatest poets in the English language. I find his work very scary and disturbing and sexy and beautiful.")

"Who's that?" I say, pointing at the photograph.

"That's my mother," says Thom. "With me, as a baby."

Thom's parents were divorced when he was eight or nine, and after that he was on fairly distant terms with his father (a successful journalist who went on to edit *The Daily Sketch* at the height of his career). But even before the divorce he was closer to his mother. His given name, Thomson, was the name of his mother's family, and he identified with that side of his heritage. "My mother was one of seven children, all girls," he has written, "and all of a very independent turn of mind." One of Thom's childhood memories is of his mother "wearing an orchid pinned by a brooch in the shape of a hammer and sickle.

From this distance the combination sounds like a cliché of the thirties, but it wasn't: other women wouldn't have done something so outrageous." He also recalls being lost at the age of about four in Kensington Gardens and being asked by a policeman to describe his mother. "A proud woman," the little boy answered.

When Thom was fifteen his mother committed suicide; he and his younger brother found the body. For most of his writing life he could not directly address this fact. (In his one published fragment of autobiography, the tragedy takes place between sentences, as it would in an E. M. Forster novel.) Then, in 1992, Gunn published a poem called "The Gas-Poker," which begins:

> *Forty-eight years ago*
> *—Can it be forty-eight*
> *Since then?—they forced the door*
> *Which she had barricaded*
> *With a full bureau's weight*
> *Lest anyone find, as they did,*
> *What she had blocked it for.*

The two boys who are the poem's "they"—"Elder and younger brother"—go outside to walk and cry and try to understand what has happened to them. Then:

> *Coming back off the grass*
> *To the room of her release*

THE AMATEUR

They who had been her treasures
Knew to turn off the gas,
Take appropriate measures,
Telephone the police.

Borrowing the strategy he had used in the poems
about LSD, Gunn relied on rhyme and meter to organize
an experience that would otherwise be incomprehensi-
bly, uncontrollably painful. "Take appropriate measures":
it's in the very impersonality of the phrase (echoing, as
it does, the expressive "who had been her treasures") that
the sense of personal loss comes through most strongly.

"The surprising thing about one's dead," Thom Gunn
said to me many years ago, "is that your relationship with
them can change over time. Even after they've been dead
for years, you still find your feelings about them changing, or growing. And that makes them seem to alter, too."

I asked him recently if he still feels that way. "Yes," he
said. "Yes. Exactly. The longer people are dead, the more
your relationship with them changes."

ELEGY FOR MARIO SAVIO

H e wasn't, in the strictest sense of the word, an author. He never published a book. He was even a bit wary of publishing, as I learned when I set out to print one of his commemorative speeches in a 1995 issue of *The Threepenny Review*. He confessed to me, with an almost painful nervousness, that he hesitated to engage in any sort of publication for fear of losing the copyright, and when I assured him that I was acquiring one-time rights only, and that he would retain all further copyright, he explained to me the source of his anxiety. Early in his career he had allowed some of his speeches to be published, only to discover that in doing so he had unwittingly given away the rights to them. That such a thing was possible—that he could be deprived of the possession of his own sentences—surprised and wounded him. He had thought of speech as something free; it shocked him to see it treated as a salable commodity, a product divorced from its maker.

But if he was not an author in the book sense of the word, Mario Savio was nonetheless a poet. He was the only political figure of my era for whom language truly mattered. He was the last American, perhaps, who believed that civil, precisely worded, expressive, emotionally truthful exhortation could bring about significant change. He was the only person I have ever seen or met who gave political speech the weight and subtlety of literature. The irony is that his power lay entirely in the spoken word, so that what he said on any given occasion could never quite be captured in print. His voice—the very sound of it, its accent and emphasis and pitch—was physically a part of the meaning of his words. And with his death on November 6, 1996, that voice was silenced.

I hardly knew Mario Savio (and in this respect I was unusual in Berkeley, where half the population seemed to consider him an old friend). I met him only once, talked to him on the phone about printing his speech, saw him occasionally at a rally or a memorial service. I wasn't even around to hear his fiery early speeches, because in 1964, when he was making history as part of Berkeley's Free Speech Movement, I was still a junior high school student in Palo Alto, down on the quiet Peninsula, away from all the action. But I heard about him then, and when, twenty or thirty years later, I saw videotapes of his speeches, I instantly understood what I had missed. Like most people my age, I had heard an endless number of

protest speeches in the late Sixties and early Seventies,
but I had never heard political speech like Mario Savio's.
He spoke without notes of any kind, and he spoke at
length, directly addressing his audience with passion and
imagination. But that, in a way, was the least of it. The
sentences he spoke were complicated and detailed, with
clauses and metaphors and little byways of digression
that together added up to a coherent grammatical whole.
When he spoke, he seemed inspired—literally so, as if he
were breathing thought through language. That's how
natural it seemed.

Apparently he had stammered in his youth, so much
so that he was nearly unable to deliver his own valedic-
torian speech in high school. It was not until he came to
Berkeley that he found his gift, and he was to lose and
find it more than once after that, for the times weren't always right for someone of his strengths and vulnerabil-
ities. He brought an innocence to the world—a pure,
ingenuous, trusting sense of righteousness and compas-
sion—that the world was ill equipped to handle. Sometimes, even before he died, I would think of him as a
sainted Dostoyevskian fool, like Prince Myshkin in *The
Idiot*. Since I have always been a confirmed atheist, such
thoughts do not come easily to me, but when I think of
Mario Savio I find it difficult to conceive of him in any
other way. It goes against my grain to think in terms of
martyrdom, but something of the martyr's unusual

power is there in his story. He did not set out to be a martyr, certainly, but he was willing to lose in the name of justice; there were more important things to him than winning. "We are moving right now in a direction which one could call creeping barbarism," he said in 1994. "But if we do not have the benefit of the belief that in the end we will win, then we have to be prepared on the basis of our moral insight to struggle even if we do *not* know that we are going to win."

He was gentle, even to those who behaved brutally, and he was decent, even when he was angry. In 1964, when he clambered up on a police car to protest the arrest of a fellow student, he took off his shoes first so he wouldn't damage the car. Such gentleness did not prevail in American politics. In that sense, Mario Savio had no direct inheritors. His was a political pathway that led nowhere, a dead end in our evolutionary development. This is our loss. We were unable to learn what he had to teach us, because we were unable to conceive of political language that could be truthful rather than just persuasive. Mario Savio's literary gifts were intimately tied to his political perceptions: he could not have cared about fairness or equality or humanity in exactly the way he did without caring about language in exactly the way he did. Yet such precision came, in the practical world of politics, to seem irrelevant, inconvenient, worse than useless. A complexity of language meant a complexity of thought, and a complexity of thought meant that you couldn't win an election. But Mario Savio's politics weren't just about winning elections; they were about changing the way people thought about each other and the world.

He died of a heart attack, shortly after a debate with the president of his university over the issue of raising student fees. (Ironically, and typically, it was the *president's* heart he was worried about when they finished the stressful debate.) Raising student fees at the state university would, he argued, make it increasingly difficult for poor kids to go to college. He knew exactly what he was talking about: Mario Savio, the son of a machinist, had earned all his degrees at state universities. The student-fee problem was something that everyone else at the university probably would have swept under the carpet, if Mario Savio hadn't singlehandedly turned it into a cause. He was always making extra trouble for himself, finding causes where other people found only problems to ignore. He couldn't help himself.

"At least he died fighting," said my husband, who works at the same university where Mario Savio taught remedial math, formal logic, and physics. "There are worse ways to go."

"I think it's more that there was no other way for him to live," I said.

His death has moved and upset me more than I could have predicted, considering how little I knew him. I feel

as if something very old and valuable, something ir-
replaceable, has been taken away from me and destroyed.
I feel as if the last surviving member of a rare and beautiful species has disappeared from the earth. I take the
loss personally, and I long to hear the kinds of comforting words that Mario Savio himself could have provided,
in his secular-humanist, quasi-religious, saintly-priestly
way. But the only voice that could have offered such comfort is one that we won't, any of us, hear again.

MY IMAGINARY NEW YORK LIFE

F or many years I thought that living in California was just a phase. One day I would move to New York and become a grown-up: a *real* editor, a *real* writer, in the place where such careers had both a tangible and a mythical force.

This was unlike the other, briefer, imaginary habitations that we all occupy at various times. When my son, for instance, first saw Amsterdam at the age of ten, he said, "I could live here." He had taken instant possession of it and reserved it for one of his possible futures, just as I had fallen for other beautiful cities: Edinburgh, London, Jerusalem, Perugia. I was reminded of this fleeting habit when, a few years ago, I revisited Boston and sat in a North End café with my family. Looking around at the old red-brick buildings, I remembered the college student who had planned to take an apartment here someday. "Planned" is perhaps too strong a word: she had a vision of herself living alone in such an apartment, a vision that came to her during a Sunday jaunt from Cambridge. Recalling that vision, I was surprised to discover how thoroughly that young woman—at least, that particular aspect of that young woman—had ceased to exist.

But the lure of New York was stronger. Many of my friends from college had settled there, and in the years after college I would go to visit them. At the beginning we were all rather poor, in a bohemian and generally undesperate way. One of the apartments I sometimes stayed in on my visits had, as its only guest area, a closet-like space we called "the Raskolnikov room." On one winter's visit I became so sick, lying there in the Raskolnikov room, that I had to be rescued by family friends living on Park Avenue. Propped up on the white couch of their eighteenth-floor living room, wrapped in a mohair blanket and sipping chamomile tea, I looked out the window and thought: I am too young and poor to live in New York now; I'll wait until my friends have become rich and famous before I move here. (I can't imagine why I thought the wealth and fame of my friends would automatically be transferred to *me*, but in our twenties, in the Seventies, we were all more prone to confusions of that sort.)

And then later, when I began to have literary business to transact, I would come to New York at least once or twice every year. By this time my friends *had* become richer and more famous, and I had nicer places to stay. Also, I had more of a reason for being in the city: a book

critics' meeting to attend, a *Threepenny* reading to host,
a P E N conference to drop in on. I was not an insider to
the world of New York's literary life, but I was no longer
a complete outsider.

It wasn't that my New York life was all forward movement. There were plenty of setbacks. I remember one
December when I was occupying a borrowed apartment
on Barrow Street, and my first book had just come out to
virtually no reviews, and I felt a bit of a fraud and a bit of
a failure, and every taxi I took seemed to be driven by an
aspiring novelist or an aspiring musician, to the point
where New York seemed bursting at the seams with aspiring types like me: we were all aspiration, with nothing much to show for it. And I remember another visit,
summer this time, when I was grumpily steaming down
Fifth Avenue (no doubt having failed to interest any pub-
lishers in advertising in *The Threepenny Review*, or any
bookstores in stocking it), and a street vendor shoved an
"I ❤ N Y" button in my face, causing me to snarl, "I *don't*
love New York! I *hate* New York!"

But these occasions were relatively few. Mostly what
I remember is wonderful October evenings—sometimes
unseasonably warm, sometimes with a slight chill in the
air—when I would venture out from a friend's Upper
West Side apartment into that glorious New York twilight, with the lights just coming on inside people's
rooms and the convivial sidewalk tables clustered to-

gether on Broadway or Columbus, and it would seem that everything was possible.

Years passed. Many things happened to me: a husband, a child, a brief brush with a rather frightening form of skin cancer, the acquisition of a house I loved. I became, willy-nilly, increasingly attached to my life in the form it had taken, ever more firmly embedded in a particular place. I skipped a couple of trips to New York; we went, that year, to London instead, and I transferred some of my imaginings to that older (but, to me, also newer) metropolis.

And then, just a few months ago, I was back in New York for a weeklong stay. I had a lot of time on my hands, and I spent it visiting with friends: lunch in the Village, dinner in Gramercy Park, breakfast at the Algonquin, cocktails near Lincoln Center. One evening I went to have a drink with a friend on the Upper West Side, the woman with whom I had often stayed in earlier years. As I was leaving her apartment, I suddenly had one of those moments of clarity, those rare moments in which you become aware of the extent to which you are no longer the person you once were.

It had been a beautiful, sunny day in May, and the light was golden at that hour, as it always was in my memories of the best New York days. I was going to meet another friend for dinner a few blocks away, and as I swung down Columbus I expected to have a recurrence of that old the-world-was-all-before-me feeling. But I didn't. What I had instead was the sense that a life which had once been all possibility had now congealed, to a large extent, into actuality. It was not a bad life—in fact, it was a very good life, one that I wouldn't have changed for anything. But that was part of the problem, part of the awareness. Once change had represented promise. Now it was merely threat. I had made my choices, and I was pleased with how they had turned out, but the best I could hope for, it seemed to me at that moment, was to hold on to what I already had. The world was *not* all before me; at least half of it was now behind.

I suppose you would call this a sense of mortality, of impending death. But I did not feel it that way. Death, after all, is a change ("the last new experience," as Arnold Bennett has eloquently called it), whereas what I had suddenly become aware of was stasis. I was not, after all, going to have a New York life. I had become pretty much the person I had planned to be, but without ever moving to New York. Apparently the New York self was not as essential a part of me as I had once imagined. She had somehow been jettisoned by circumstances along the way, and it was only when I turned around to find her, there on Columbus Avenue, that I found out she was gone.